礼记图典
The Illustrated Book of Rites

编　绘　周春才

翻　译　贺　军

审　订　Hannah Deacon

 海豚出版社
DOLPHIN BOOKS

First Edition 2006

ISBN 7-80138-519-5

© Dolphin Books, Beijing, 2006
Published by Dolphin Books
24 Baiwanzhuang Road, Beijing 100037, China

Printed in the People's Republic of China

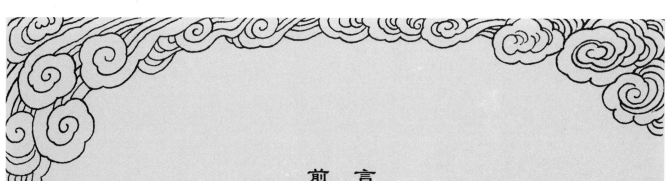

前　言

古代社会的"礼"是中国的先民在"天人合一"背景下，通过取法自然而制定的，并以此获得了形而上的依据。"礼"，是中国文化的象征与标志。

中国的礼仪文化自黄帝肇始、周公完成，孔子承前启后，作为中国人的灵魂主宰，已经绵延了数千年。历史上，它曾是中国人"修身、齐家、治国、平天下"的知识渊薮，而时至今日以及可以预期的未来，"礼"的精神仍是中国人处理人与人、国与国、民族与民族、宗教与宗教之间关系时不可或缺的圭臬。

就一个民族而言，没有一个众望所归的信念与原则是不可想象的，数千年来，恰恰是"礼"为中国人提供了具有普遍意义的价值观、伦理观、道德观和人生观，它赋予了人们艺术化的语言，仪式化的举止，和谐融洽的环境，以及自信恢弘的气度。

对个人而言，"礼"则为人们提供了一条提升个人尊严，实现自我价值，让一生过得从容，使心灵找到家园的蹊径通衢。

Foreword

Guided by the idea that "man is an integral part of nature," the forefathers of the Chinese people created the rite of ancient China by following the rules governing heaven and earth. "Rite" has become the symbol of Chinese culture ever since.

In China, rite, as a cultural form, was started by Huang Di and completed by Lord Zhou. Confucius was a key figure who carried forward the rich heritage of rite and contributed to it many new ideas. Rite has existed for more than several thousand years, serving as the governing force of the souls of the Chinese people. It gave rise to the Confucian proverb "cultivate yourself, put your family in order, run the local government well, and bring peace to the entire country." Even today, and in the foreseeable future, the spirit of the rite will remain an indispensable criterion for the Chinese people as they handle the relations between different people, different countries, different races, and different religions.

It is inconceivable for a nation not to have a faith or principle with widespread support. Over the past several thousand years, rite has provided the Chinese with values, ethics, morals and a world outlook in general. It gives us an artistic language, ceremonious bearing, harmonious environment, and a confident and noble manner.

For individuals, rite provided the path on which one could enhance one's self-esteem, realize one's values, lead a peaceful life and find a home for one's heart.

Contents

引 言

　　古代社会的礼，是我们的祖先为维护"天人合一"这一生态理念而制定的。正是赖于这一以和谐为最高宗旨的理念，礼才可以由道德层面得到提升，进而逾越宗教，使我们这个幅员辽阔、人口众多的国家得以维系其间，繁衍生息，并创造出了博大精深的中华传统道德与文化。

Introduction

In ancient China our forefathers created rite to safeguard the ecological idea that "man is an integral part of nature." Because this theory considers harmony to be its highest purpose, rite is therefore elevated from the level of morals to surpass religion and become a binding force of our vast and populous country. With it, people lived and developed, and created an extensive Chinese culture with profound traditional morals.

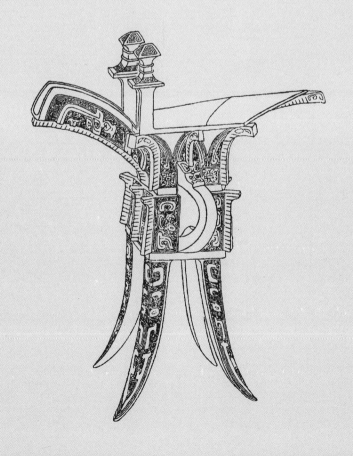

礼，作为人类社会发展的产物和文明的标志，在很早以前就产生了，经过不断完善，至周代从内容到形式已经形成了一整套完备的体系。中国素称"礼仪之邦"，其基础就是由那时候奠定的。

Rite came into existence very early as a product of the social development of mankind and as a symbol of civilization. After continuous improvements, it had formed a complete system in both form and content by the Zhou Dynasty some 3,000 years ago. China has been known as a "state of rites" and its foundations were laid at that time.

礼

Rite

说到礼，就必须从儒学谈起，儒学是孔子在二千五百多年前创立的。人们通常所讲的中国传统文化，就是指作为主流文化的儒学。

It is difficult to discuss rites without reference to Confucianism as they were created by Confucius more than 2,500 years ago. Traditional Chinese culture, as it is considered today, refers to Confucianism that had been the main-stream culture in ancient China.

这一思想体系的标志就是本书所要阐述的"礼"。
The symbol of this ideological system is rites, which we are going to explain in this book.

儒家的核心思想是充满同情和友爱、以及深切的人文关怀的"仁"，即所谓"仁者爱人"；表现形式就是"礼"。
The fundamental principle of Confucianism is "benevolence," which includes sympathy, brotherhood and humanitarian concern. The benevolent love people, and the form of expression of this benevolence is the rites.

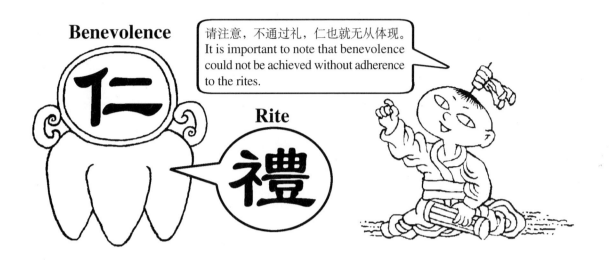

Benevolence

请注意，不通过礼，仁也就无从体现。
It is important to note that benevolence could not be achieved without adherence to the rites.

Rite

以"礼"为标志的儒家伦理道德观念对人们的意识形态影响尤其巨大，正是它将我们这个幅员辽阔、人口众多的国家凝聚为一体，形成一个闻名于世的礼仪之邦的。
The Confucian ethics and morals with the rites as its symbol have great influence on people's ideology. Throughout history, the rites have united China, making it a "land of rites" well-known all over the world.

中国有礼义之大，故称夏；有服章之美，谓之华。作为传统文化的元素，"礼"为整个中华民族构筑了独具特色的价值体系，为我们提供了行为与思维的准则。

"China is sometimes referred to as Xia because of its rites; it is also referred to as Hua because of its fine clothing and beautiful jade designs." As the foremost element of traditional culture, rites formed a distinctive system of values for the Chinese nation and provided norms for our actions and thoughts.

一方面，它对社会具有协调和稳定的重要作用。
On the one hand, rites play the important role of coordinating and stabilizing society.

臣止于敬，
Officials were required to be respectful.

君止于仁。
Monarchs were supposed to be benevolent.

父止于慈，子止于孝。
A father was supposed to be kind-hearted while a son was supposed to be dutiful.

人与人之间止于信等等。
People were expected to be trustworthy.

言必信，
To be true in word,

行必果。
and resolute in deed.

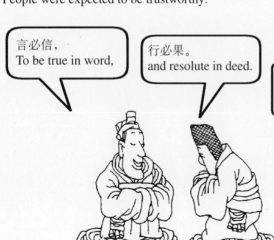

即"礼"对人是一种约束。
Rites were a restriction to people.

另一方面，"礼"又是达到"仁"这一理想和境界的载体，即人格提升和完善的必要途径。而人格完善则是儒家的毕生追求，即终极目的。

On the other hand, rites were the medium through which one attained the ideal and the superior realm of " benevolence." In other words, it is the path one has to travel if he wants to build and improve his character. For Confucianists, the improvement of one's character is a lifelong pursuit and an ultimate goal.

Benevolence

这个终极目的不是禁欲中的彼岸，也不是苦海里的涅槃，而是对自我本性的回归，对自然法则的皈依。是人与人、与物、与自然之间无可名状的和谐与融洽。

The ultimate objective is not the other shore to be reached when practicing asceticism. Nor is it a nirvana in the void of misery. Rather, it is a return to one's very nature and a regression to the natural laws. It is the inexplicable harmony between one person and another, between man and animals, between man and nature.

所以"仁"又不仅指同情和友爱，还同时被赋予了心灵归宿的终极内含。

Besides the implication of sympathy and brotherhood, benevolence also has the attribute of being the ultimate sanctuary of the mind.

就一个民族而言，没有一个众望所归的信念与原则是难以想象的，数千年来，恰恰是"礼"为我们提供了具有普遍意义的价值观、伦理观、道德观、人生观。它曾赋予了我们艺术化的语言，仪式化的举止，和谐融洽的环境，以及自信恢弘的气度。

It is inconceivable for a nation not to have a faith or principle with widespread support. Over the past several thousand years, rites have provided us with values, ethics, morals and a world outlook in general. They give us an artistic language, ceremonious bearing, harmonious environment, and a confident and noble manner.

礼记图典

6

对个人来说，"礼"则为人们设计了一条提升个人尊严，实现自我价值，让一生过得从容，使心灵找到家园的蹊径通衢。

For individuals, rites provided the path on which one could enhance one's self-esteem, realize one's values, lead a peaceful life and find a home for one's heart.

按"礼"的精神去生活，依自然的法则来做事，就随时可以步入这一境界。

Lead your life in the spirit of rites and do things in accordance with natural laws and you will enter this realm with ease.

《礼记》中为"礼"下定义的地方很多，但最重要的一个原则是取法天地，效仿自然(见作者的另一部作品《易经图典》)。
There are many parts in *The Book of Rites* that give definitions to rites. Yet the most important principle is to follow the examples of heaven and earth and imitate nature (Refer to *The Illustrated Book of Changes* by the author).

河图洛书就是对宇宙功能的总体把握，对自然谱系的实录，是中华文明的统一场。
The River Map and the Luo Writing is about how to have a general command of the functions of the universe. It is a factual record of the nature's system of change and development. It is the unifying field of Chinese civilization.

然后将人的行为、思维，乃至上层建筑的所有领域都自觉地纳入其中。这一点与"天人合一"的世界观是一致的。
With it, man's actions, thinking and all realms of the superstructure will be automatically included. In this regard it is in conformity with the world outlook that "man is an integral part of nature."

所以"礼"又是不与人的本性相悖离的，因为"礼也者，理也"。在儒家的学说中，"礼"的本质是可以用数学语言来描述的，因而就原理而言，"礼"中不包含有超自然的因素。
Therefore rite is not contrary to human nature, since it is a system based on rational knowledge. According to Confucian theories, the nature of rite can be described by using numerical language. So as far as the tenet is concerned, rite does not contain supernatural elements.

正是赖于"天人合一"世界观的指导，"礼"才可以从道德这一层面得到提升，进而兼具宗教的统摄功能。
Because of the guiding principle of the world outlook that "man is an integral part of nature," rite is elevated from the level of morality to have the additional commanding function of religion.

这是由于道德常常是乏味的、缺乏约束力的。
This is because morality is often boring and lacks binding force.

而对自然的敬畏和自身本性的感悟则会使人自觉地克勤克俭，无出其外。
The fear of nature and the awareness of one's innate self will make one work hard and live a prudent life without going beyond the limits.

以自然立约，铸人生法度。
Following nature to set out the moral standards of life.

因而在以宗教作为灵魂主宰的世界各民族当中，唯独中华民族选择了"礼"，这一充满理性精神、体现自然法则的机杼，用以维系天地之间。
Almost all nationalities in the world use religion as the governing force of people's souls, but the Chinese people have chosen rite — a concept full of rational spirit and reflecting the laws of nature — as the union of everything between heaven and earth.

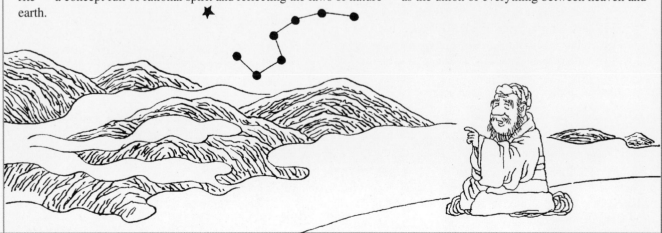

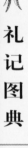

由此可见，作为涵盖面更广的固有文化，《礼记》中的"礼"和我们现在通常所讲的礼貌、礼节等含义是不尽相同的。如果以此来衡量周代的"礼"，就会有许多问题找不到答案。

We can see that as part of an indigenous culture that covers a much wider range, rite as described in *The Book of Rites* is not quite the same thing as manners or etiquette that we refer to today. If we used today's definition of li (rite) to judge the rite of the Zhou Dynasty, we would be unable to come up with answers to many questions.

Rite

而这恰恰可以使我们追溯今日的许多社会现象，乃至整个民族的心路历程，甚至影响到我们对未来生活的判断。

By studying *The Book of Rites* we can observe many social phenomena of today and trace the course of development of our nation. It will also influence our judgment on our lives in the future.

同时，它所形成的众多典故为我们提供了丰富的常识与知识，可以用来提高我们的文化素养。

In addition, many of the literary allusions from this book provide information about a wide range of things, adding to our cultural attainment.

而其所汇集的许多对自然与社会的真知灼见，则更是对民族自信心的回归与重塑大有助益。

Moreover, *The Book of Rites* contains many deep insights into nature and society, which will help the Chinese people regain and rebuild their confidence as a nation.

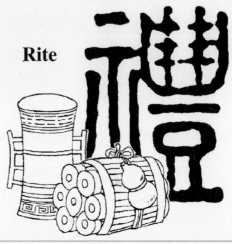

Rite

两千多年来，中国的仁人志士无不以此作为"修身、齐家、治国、平天下"的思想知识渊薮，它所代表的价值标准和思想观念，早已渗透到社会的各个阶层和角落，溶进了民族的血液之中。历史上，特别是近代以来，尽管人们对其褒贬有加，但它对于国家的凝聚、民族的复兴、人格的完善而言，还是无可替代的，认识到这一点，就可以发掘《礼记》这一文化宝藏了。

For more than 2,000 years in China, public-spirited people who follow the Confucian proverb "cultivate yourself, put your family in order, run the local government well, and bring peace to the entire country" all considered *The Book of Rites* the source of ideas and knowledge. The values and ideology it represents have permeated all social stratums and have been ingrained into the minds of the nation. Although historically people have had different opinions about the value of the book — especially in modern history when some people expressed negative opinions about the book — it is still irreplaceable in terms of the unity of the country, rejuvenation of the nation and improvement of one's character. With this in mind, we can begin to examine *The Book of Rites*, the cultural treasure of ancient China.

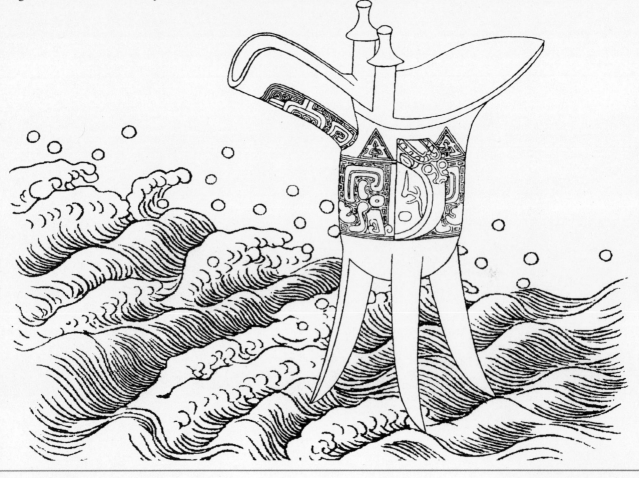

曲 礼

曲礼之"曲"，即细小委曲之意，引申为日常起居、饮食、待人接物中的礼节和各种应知应懂的称谓常识等。在古代，有"十年，朝夕学幼仪"之说，就是讲，儿童到十岁时，就要学习这些礼仪，用以规范其行为、陶冶其情操，从而成为一个有道德修养的谦谦君子。文章分上下两篇。

Rites to Be Learned When Young

Qu li, or trivial rites, refer to etiquettes governing a person's daily routine, including eating, social intercourse and the proper way of addressing other people. In ancient China, children were supposed to learn and know these etiquettes by the age of ten. These etiquettes served as norms for their behaviors, refining their attitude and making them gracious gentlemen with high moral standards. The article is divided into two parts.

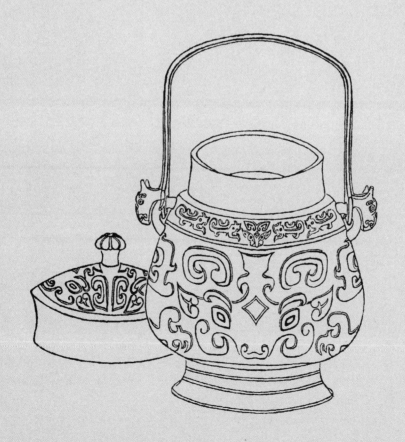

《曲礼》曰：

毋不敬，俨若思，

安定辞。安民哉！

敖不可长，欲不可

从，志不可满，

乐不可极。

《曲礼》上说：一切行为都要以敬为准则。
Qu li says that respectability should be standard behavior.

要端庄持重，若有所思。说话要从容明确，这样才可使百姓信服呀！
One should act in a dignified and prudent manner, looking pensive. When speaking, one should be calm and specific. Only in this way can you convince your audience.

不可有傲慢之心，欲望不可放纵。
Never be arrogant. Don't indulge in your desires.

志向不可以自满，享乐则应适可而止。
One should never feel complacent in pursuing one's ambitions. Avoid excessive indulgence in creature comforts.

忘记先生的教导了？
Forgotten the teacher's instructions?

賢者狎而敬之，畏而愛之。愛而知其惡，憎而知其善。積而能散，安安而能遷。臨財毋苟得，臨難毋苟免。很毋求勝，分毋求多。疑事毋質，直而勿有。

对有德行的君子要亲近并敬重他，畏服而又爱慕他。
Admire gentlemen with integrity; show awe and respect for them.

对所爱的人，要分辨出他的恶。
Find the evil in a person you love.

对所厌烦的人，要能看出他的优点。
Find the strong points in a person you loathe.

能积聚财富，也能分派财富。
Be able to amass wealth and distribute wealth.

既能随遇而安，又能适应变化。
Be able to live in peace and comfort and adapt to change as well.

遇到财物不可随便取得，遇到危难不可随便逃避。
Don't take wealth that doesn't belong to you. Don't run away from dangers.

意见相反的，不要压服人家。
Don't force people with different opinions to yield to you.

您慢慢说。
Speak your mind.

分配财物，不可要求多得。
Don't ask for the lion's share when distributing wealth.

自己不明白的事，不要乱做证明。陈述自己的意见，让对方抉择，不要强加于人。
Don't confirm anything you don't understand. State your views and let the other person make the decision. Don't force your opinions on others.

道德仁义，非礼不成，教训正俗，非礼不备。分争辩讼，非礼不决。君臣上下，父子兄弟，非礼不定。宦学事师，非礼不亲。班朝治军，莅官行法，非礼威严不行。祷祠祭祀，供给鬼神，非礼不诚不庄。

道德仁义，是通过"礼"获得的。教学和训导是用来纠正社会习俗的，如果没有"礼"，不免要有缺陷。
Virtue and morality cannot be implemented without rites. Teaching and instruction are used to correct social customs. Without rites, there will be defects.

分辨事理，如果不以"礼"为标准，就无从判断。
You cannot judge right from wrong without rite as the criterion.

君臣、上下、父子、兄弟，如果不通过"礼"，就无法界定名分。
Without rite the social status of monarch and ministers, superiors and subordinates, father and son, and brothers can not be clearly defined.

学习政务，研究学问和侍奉师长，如果没有礼仪标准，就不会融洽。

When it comes to studying administrative affairs, engaging in scholarships and respecting elders, there would be no harmony if there was no criterion for the rites.

朝廷的官阶和军队的治理，就职任事，执行法令，如果缺了礼法，就会失去威严，不能使人服从。

With regard to the rankings of officials in the court, the management of military affairs, the appointing of officials and implementation of law and order, without rites, there would be no authoritative power to govern the people.

所有供奉祖先和神灵的祭祀之礼，如果不按一定的仪式，就失去诚意和恭敬。

All sacrificial offerings to ancestors and spirits would lose their sincerity and respect if they were not conducted in accordance with specific ritual procedures.

是故圣人作，为礼以教人，使人以有礼，知自别于禽兽。大上贵德，其次务施报。礼尚往来，往而不来，非礼也；来而不往，亦非礼也。人有礼则安，无礼则危。故曰礼者不可不学也。

所以圣人出现后，制定礼仪以教化人民，使人掌握了礼法，知道自己不是禽兽。

After the sage emerges, he formulates rites to teach his people, making them realize that they are different from beasts.

上古时代的人们注重"德"，以后就讲究给别人以恩惠和报答别人的恩惠。

People in antiquity put emphasis on virtue. It was considered a virtue to grant other people favors and repay others for their favors.

"礼"提倡"施"与"报"，凡是受别人恩惠而不报答，则不合乎"礼"。受人报答而没有恩惠于人的，也不合乎"礼"。

Rites advocate granting and returning favors. To receive favors without paying them back does not conform to rites; Nor is getting others' repayment without granting them favors first sanctioned by rites.

人有了"礼"，才能得到安定，失去了"礼"，就要发生倾覆。

With rites, one will live in peace. Without it, life will be turned upside down.

所以说，"礼"是不可以不学的。
So, it is essential that everyone learn the rites.

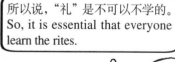

夫礼者，自卑而尊人。虽负贩者，必有尊也，而况富贵乎？富贵而知好礼，则不骄不淫；贫贱而知好礼，则志不慑。

"礼"的精神，在于克制自己，尊重他人。
The spirit of rites is to restrain oneself and respect others.

即使贩夫走卒中，也一定会有值得尊敬的人，更不必说富贵一族了。
Good honest people can be found not only among the rich and influential but even amongst poorer tradesmen and workers.

富贵的人懂得爱好"礼"，才不至于骄奢淫逸。
When understanding the rites, the rich and powerful will not indulge in dissipation and debauchery.

贫贱的人懂得爱好"礼"，则志向不至于卑怯困惑。
When understanding the rites, the poor and underprivileged will not feel diffident and perplexed.

烛不见跋，尊容之前不叱狗。让食不唾。

侍坐于君子，君子欠伸，撰杖履，视日蚤莫，侍坐者请出矣。

侍坐于君子，君子问更端，则起而对。

侍坐于君子，若有告者曰：少间，愿有复也，则左右屏而待。

"烛不见跋"即不要见到照明物的灰烬，古以火炬、油烛照明，跋即照明物的残本。本句是说在灯盏没有燃尽之前，要相机告辞。
When paying a visit, take leave of your host before you outstay your welcome.

在所尊敬的客人面前，不要叱喝驱狗。
Don't shout at the dog in front of a respectable guest.

还有孩子，也不要叱喝！
Don't shout at children, either.

主人奉上的食物，即使不可口，也不要嫌弃。
Even if the food prepared by your host is not to your taste, do not show your dislike.

味道好极了！
Delicious!

陪伴尊长者谈话，若是见到尊长者打呵欠、伸懒腰、摆弄拐杖和鞋子、看时间的早晚，侍坐者就要告辞退出了。
During a conversation with an elderly person, if he begins to yawn, stretch his limbs, play with his walking stick or shoes, or look at the time, then it is time to take your leave.

陪伴长者，如长者忽然问到另一件事，则要起立回答，表示重视和敬意。
When you are keeping an elderly person company, if that person asks you something new, you are supposed to stand up before giving your answer to show that you are serious and respect him.

陪伴尊长，如果有人进来说：打扰一下，有事汇报。
If you are keeping an elderly person company and someone interrupts to report something,

这时侍坐者就应退避到一旁静候。
Then you should move to the side and wait in silence.

曲礼下

国君死
社稷，
大夫死众，
士死制。

国君当为保卫社稷而死。
The monarch shall die to defend the sheji (country).

"社"，是为祭五土之神而设。"稷"是为祭五谷之神而设。稷非土无以生，土非稷无以见生生之效，故古人祭社必及稷。社稷不屋而坛，社坛在东，稷坛在西，象征国家。
She refers to the altar erected to offer sacrifices to the god of the five-colour lands; ji refers to the altar erected to offer sacrifices to the god of the five grains. The sacrificial offering ceremony to both gods was always held at the same time, with the she altar in the east and the ji altar in the west. Together they represent the country.

赤 Red
青 Blue
黄 Yellow
白 White
黑 Black

（社）She

（稷）Ji

大夫当公而忘私(不死宗庙)，为民而死。
Senior officials shall work for the public interest and die for the people.

士当为国尽职而死。
Ordinary officials shall work diligently to fulfill their duties for the country until death.

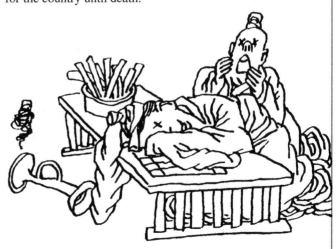

天子当依而立，诸侯北面而见天子曰觐。天子当宁而立，诸公东面，诸侯西面曰朝。诸侯未及期相见曰遇，相见于郤地曰会。诸侯使大夫问于诸侯曰聘，约信曰誓，莅牲曰盟。

天子站在黑白相间的屏风前面，诸侯北向朝见天子称"觐"。天子站在正门当中，诸公东向，诸侯西向朝见天子，叫"朝"。
Dukes or princes are received by the Son of Heaven (the emperor), who stands in front of a black-and-white screen in the north. This is called jin. If his majesty stands in the middle of the main entrance while dukes stand facing east and princes stand facing west, this is called chao.

诸侯未到约定的时间相见称为"遇"。在两国中间之地相见，称为"会"。
When a duke encounters another duke before the time of appointment, it is called yu. When they meet at a place between the two countries, it is called hui.

诸侯派遣大夫访问诸侯，称为"聘"。
When a duke dispatches a senior official to pay a visit to another duke, it is called pin.

写下彼此共同遵守的条约，称为"誓"。
The writing of an agreement that both sides will adhere to is called shi.

杀牛歃血保证所说的话，称为"盟"。
Having an ox killed and drinking its blood as a guarantee that you will keep your promise is called meng.

天子之妃曰后，
诸侯曰夫人，
大夫曰孺，
士曰妇人，
庶人曰妻。

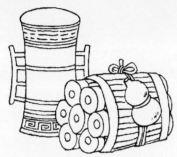

天子的配偶称为"后"。妃即天子的配偶，后即天子的正妻。
The emperor's spouse is called hou.

诸侯的配偶称为"夫人"。夫即扶意。
A duke's spouse is called furen.

大夫的配偶称"孺人"。孺即属意。
A senior official's spouse is called ruren.

我抗议

士的配偶称"妇人"。妇即服意。
A scholar's spouse is called furen (different Chinese characters from the furen above).

庶人的配偶称为"妻"。妻即齐意。
A common folk's spouse is called qi.

凡挚：天子鬯，诸侯
圭，卿羔，大夫雁，
士雉，庶人之挚匹，
童子委挚而退。
野外军中无挚，
以缨、拾、矢可也。
妇人之挚，椇、榛、
脯、枣、栗。

一般相见时所用的礼品是：天子以黑黍所酿，芳香的具有调畅上下之功的鬯酒。
Gifts are presented when people meet: the Son of Heaven presents a fine wine made from millet.

和以郁金之草称郁鬯，不以郁和则直称为鬯。
Tumeric may or may not be added to the wine.

诸侯用命圭以示身份。
Dukes and princes present jade tablets to show their status.

卿用羔羊，取其群而不党、洁白清素之意。
Ministers present lambs because lambs never form a clique to pursue selfish interests. Furthermore, the white of the lamb's coat is considered a sign of integrity.

大夫用雁，取其知时，且飞行有序。
Other senior officials present wild geese because they are punctual and orderly in flight.

士用雉鸡，取其性之耿介，且文饰华美。
Scholars present pheasants because they are upright with beautiful feathers.

它被捉后就会不食而死。
When a pheasant is caught, it refuses to eat and therefore dies of hunger.

庶人则用鸭，取不能飞腾，如庶人之终守耕稼。
Common folks present ducks because they cannot fly, just like the peasant who has to till the land all his life.

儿童随其所有，但不敢与成人为礼，只将礼物放于地上，便可告退。
Children present whatever they have. But they do not present gifts to adults. They just leave their gifts on the ground and walk away.

我忘记带礼物了。
I forgot to bring a gift.

在野外军中，找不到合适的礼物，用缨络、皮护袖、箭矢即可。
When you are with the troops out in the battlefield and can not find a suitable gift, you can use tassel, fur oversleeve, or arrows instead.

妇人相见时的礼品为橡子、榛子、肉干、枣子、栗子，以示诚意。
When women meet, they present acorns, hazelnuts, jerky, dates and chestnuts as an expression of sincerity.

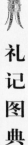

王 制

　　王制，即王者施政的纲领性文件。东汉著名经学家郑玄说："名王制者，以其记先王班爵、授禄、祭祀、养老之法度。"其中记有君主一年中所应进行的政治活动，如：封建、授田、巡守、朝觐、丧祭、田猎、学校、刑政等，为后世研究和了解古代社会提供了丰富而直观的范本。

The King's Programmatic Documents

Wangzhi refers to a king's programmatic documents for ruling the country. Zheng Xuan, an eminent Confucian scholar of the Eastern Han Dynasty (25-220AD) said, "Wangzhi refers to the rules set by the late king regarding the granting of nobility titles, paying of salaries, sacrificial offerings and supplying provisions to elderly people." It also recorded the monarch's political activities throughout the year, such as investing the nobles with fiefs, allocating land, going on inspection tours, having an audience with dukes, princes and ministers, presiding over funerals, hunting, education and handing out punishments. These documents provide a wealth of first-hand materials for later generations to study ancient societies.

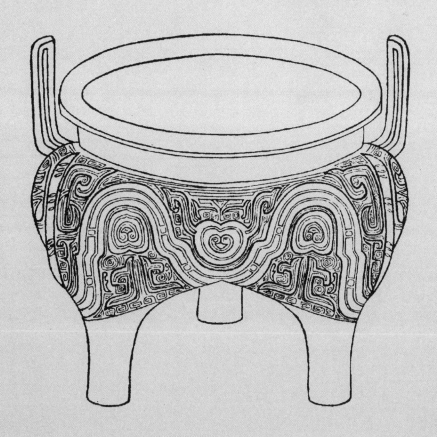

凡官民材，必先论之。论辨然后使之，任事然后爵之。位定，然后禄之。爵人于朝，与士共之。刑人于市，与众弃之。是故公家不畜刑人，大夫弗养，士遇之涂弗与言也；屏之四方，唯其所之，不及以政，示弗故生也。

凡是选用人才，必须先考核他的才德如何。答辩之后才分配工作。
When selecting qualified people, we should first test the candidates' technical skills and moral standards. After they give satisfactory replies to questions and arguments, the government will then assign them jobs.

从事所分的工作后，才正式授以爵位。位置确定后，再规定俸禄。
After starting the jobs, they will be granted titles or ranks. They will receive a salary when their positions are determined.

颁发爵位要在朝廷、士人面前公开举行。
Titles of nobility are granted publicly at court with other officials present.

处罚罪犯要在市上，使更多的人引以为戒。
Criminals are executed in a public place to serve as a warning to others.

所以政府不养育犯罪的人。
The government does not support criminals.

放逐！
They are sent into exile.

大夫也不供养犯罪的人。
Senior officials oppose criminals.

士在路上遇到犯罪的人不同他讲话。
A scholar will refuse to talk to a criminal when they run into each other in the street.

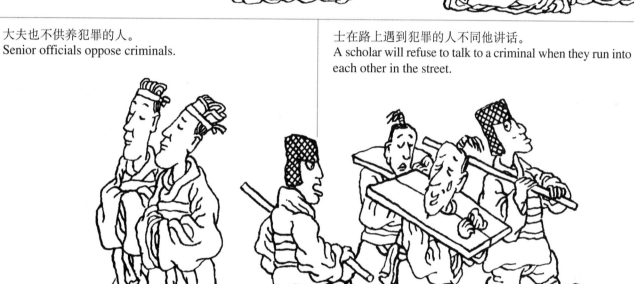

把他驱逐出境，凡他所到之处，剥夺他的公权，表示不要他活在世上。
Criminals are exiled to other countries, and deprived of their human rights wherever they go, society willing them to disappear from this world.

我们死定了！
We are doomed.

诸侯之于天子也，比年一小聘，三年一大聘，五年一朝。天子五年一巡守，岁二月，东巡守至于岱宗，柴而望祀山川。觐诸侯，问百年者就见之。命大师陈诗以观民风。命市纳贾以观民之所好恶、志淫好辟。

诸侯对于天子，每年派遣大夫为代表进行聘问，为"小聘"；每三年派遣卿为代表，进行访问，是"大聘"。
Every year, dukes and princes dispatch a senior official to pay a visit to the Son of Heaven, known as a "minor audience with the emperor." Every three years, dukes and princes dispatch a minister to pay a visit to the Son of Heaven, known as a "major audience with the emperor."

每五年诸侯亲自朝见天子。
Every five years, dukes and princes pay a personal visit to the emperor.

天子则每五年出外巡守一次，这一年二月出发，东巡到达东岳泰山。燔柴祭祀上帝并望祀山川。
The emperor goes on an inspection tour of his country once every five years. That year he sets out in February and goes eastward to Mount Tai, where he offers sacrifices to God and other river and mountain gods.

然后接见诸侯国的国君。
Then the emperor receives all the kings of the feudal states.

问候年过百岁的老人，要亲自到他们的住所去。
He personally goes to the homes of people over 100 years old to inquire about their health.

命乐官列出当地民谣，以考察民风民俗。
He orders the minister in charge of music to tell him about local folk ballads to get some idea about local customs.

一二三四五，上山打老虎。
One, two, three, four, five, go up the mountains to hunt tigers.

命商官报告物价的高低，以考察百姓的好恶。
He asks the Minister of Commerce to report local prices to assess the likes and dislikes of the common folk.

志趣是否奢华，爱好是否邪僻。
Are their interests extravagant? Are their hobbies immoral?

好质则用物贵，好奢则侈物贵。
When people are pragmatic the price of daily utensils tends to be high. If people pursue an extravagant life, the price of luxury goods will be extremely high.

命典礼，考时月，定日，同律礼乐制度、衣服正之。山川神祇有不举者为不敬，不敬者君削以地。宗庙有不顺者为不孝，不孝者君绌以爵。变礼易乐者为不从，不从者君流。革制度衣服者为畔，畔者君讨。有功德于民者，加地进律。

命典礼之官校定当地的季节，确定每日的时辰，统一律法，
The emperor orders the minister in charge of rituals to examine the seasons and different time periods of the day in that area to create a standard calendar.

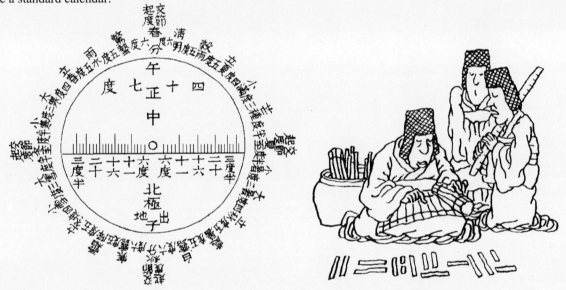

以及与之相应的礼乐制度和衣服款式。当地山川神祇的祭祀，该举行的而不举行，即为不敬。
He also determines the ritual system and what type of clothing to wear. If the lord of that area fails to offer sacrifices to the gods of mountains and rivers, which he is supposed to do, then it is an act of disrespect.

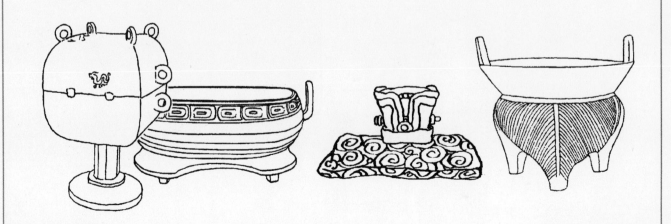

对不敬的人，就要夺削国君的封地。
The king of the feudal state who has been disrespectful will be deprived of his manor or have his land reduced.

宗庙的祭祀有失时或置换昭穆(先后)次序的，就是不孝。对不孝者，就要贬降那国君的爵位。
When sacrifices are not offered at the ancestral temple on time or not given in the correct manner, it is considered an unpious act. When this happens, the king of that feudal state will be demoted.

改变礼俗音乐的，就是不服从，如果有不服从的，就要驱逐其国君。
Changing the music of the rituals is an act of disobedience. If this happens, the king of the feudal state will be expelled.

有敢更改制度和衣服的，就是叛逆者，就要声讨其国君。
Those who dare change the rules and clothing are regarded as rebels. If this happens, the king of the feudal state will be subject to condemnation.

有功劳于人民的，要封给他们土地或增加他们的爵禄。
Those who have done meritorious service for the people will receive land, be awarded a higher ranking or an increased salary as their reward.

五月南巡守至于
南岳，如东巡
守之礼。八月，
西巡守至于
西岳，如南巡
守之礼。
十有一月，
北巡守至
于北岳，
如西巡守
之礼。归假
于祖祢。用特。

五月，向南巡守到南岳，如同东巡守的礼仪。八月，向西巡守到达西岳，如同南巡守的礼仪。十一月，向北巡守到达北岳，如同西巡守的礼仪。回到京师，到父之庙祭告，用特牲(猪牛羊)。

In May, the emperor visited the Southern Sacred Mountain where he performed the same rituals as at the Eastern Sacred Mountain. He went to the Western Sacred Mountain in August and performed the same rituals as at the Southern Sacred Mountain. He reached the Northern Sacred Mountain in November and performed the same ritual again. On his return to the capital city, he offered sacrifices at his ancestral temple, using pigs, ox and sheep all at the same time.

诸侯赐弓矢然后征，赐铁钺然后杀。赐圭瓒然后为鬯。未赐圭瓒，则资鬯于天子。天子命之教，然后为学。小学在公宫南之左，大学在郊，天子曰辟雍，诸侯曰頖宫。

诸侯要得到天子赐给的弓矢才能举兵征伐。
Without the bows and arrows granted by the Son of Heaven, dukes and princes could not go on a punitive expedition.

得到天子赐给的斧钺，才能动用诛杀的刑罚。
Without the battle-axe granted by the Son of Heaven, dukes and princes could not use the punishment of execution.

得到天子赐的玉爵，才能自行酿造祭祀降神用的鬯酒。
Only after getting the three-legged jade wine vessel from the Son of Heaven could dukes and princes brew their wine used to offer sacrifices to the gods.

在未受玉爵之前，要用鬯酒则一定要从天子那里获取。
Before the Son of Heaven granted them the three-legged jade wine vessel, dukes and princes had to ask the emperor for the wine used to offer sacrifices to gods.

天子命令诸侯办学，然后诸侯国得以设立学校。
The emperor ordered dukes and princes to run schools, so schools were established in all the feudal states.

小学设于国君之宫室的南方左边。大学设于郊外。
Primary schools were established on the left side to the south of the king's palace. Universities were established in the suburbs.

天子设的大学称为"辟雍"。"辟"为明；"雍"即和。
A college established by the emperor is called biyong. Bi means understanding and yong means harmony.

"辟雍"即取君主尊明雍和之意，在此探讨学问，研习道艺。
By naming the place biyong, the emperor wants to tell his subjects that he respects capable people and pursues harmony for the country. Biyong is an academy where people engage in academic study and pursue knowledge.

诸侯设的小学则称为"颣"。"颣"即班，是用以班治政教的。
Primary schools established by the dukes and princes were called a ban.

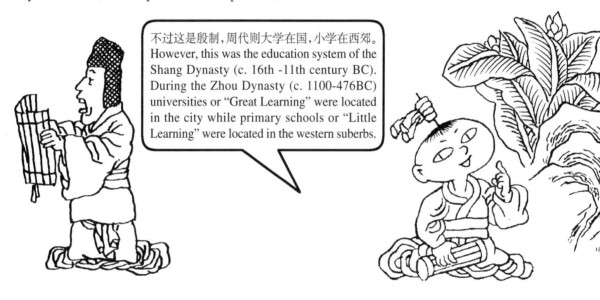

不过这是殷制，周代则大学在国，小学在西郊。
However, this was the education system of the Shang Dynasty (c. 16th -11th century BC). During the Zhou Dynasty (c. 1100-476BC) universities or "Great Learning" were located in the city while primary schools or "Little Learning" were located in the western suberbs.

一般而言，"小学"即儿童入学需先学文字，故名。汉代即指文字学，后来则引申为文字学、训诂学、音韵学的总称。
Generally speaking, children began their study by learning to read Chinese characters. Little Learning refers to philology during the Han Dynasty (206BC-220AD). Later it is used as a broader term for philology, the study of exegesis, and phonology.

"大学"的内容则为格物，致知，诚意，正心，修身，齐家，治国，平天下。
In Great Learning people pursued knowledge from the study of the physical world. More importantly, they were taught to be upright and maintain moral integrity. In brief, they were trained to be scholar-officials who cultivate themselves, put their family in order, run the local government well, and bring peace to the entire country.

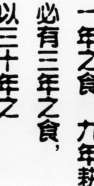

国无九年之蓄曰不足，
无六年之蓄曰急，
无三年之蓄曰国非其
国也。三年耕必有
一年之食，九年耕
必有三年之食，
以三十年之
通，虽有凶
旱水溢，
民无菜色，
然后天
子食，日
举以乐。

国家没有九年的储备，可以说不够充裕；
If a country does not have grain reserves for nine full years, it does not have enough reserves.

没有六年的储备，可以说很窘迫了；
If a country does not have grain reserves for six full years, it has a serious problem.

没有三年的储备，则已不成其为国家了。
If a country does not have grain reserves for three full years, then the country cannot be counted as a country.

耕作三年，才能得出一年的存粮。
Cultivating the land for three years will produce enough grain reserves for one year.

耕作九年，才可余出三年的存粮。
Cultivating the land for nine years will produce enough grain reserves for three years.

这样即使遇到饥荒和水旱，人民也不至于挨饿。
In this way people will not suffer from hunger in times of famine, flood or drought.

以三十年的平均数来调节盈亏，而分配预算。
Use the average amount over 30 years to regulate surplus and shortage and decide grain allocation for the coming year.

然后天子才能得以安心享受，每日听乐。
Then the emperor can enjoy music every day without worrying.

凡居民材，必因天地寒暖燥湿，广谷大川异制。民生其间者异俗，刚柔轻重迟速异齐，五味异和，器械异制，衣服异宜。修其教，不易的其俗；齐其政，不易其宜。

凡为人民部署城邑居处，必须要根据民众日常所需，当地气候的寒冷或温暖，地势的高燥或洼湿，因地制宜。
Houses are different from one place to another, depending on whether the place is hot or cold, dry or wet, whether it is in a basin or near a big river.

大盆地和大河流域，其制度不同，人民生活在不同地区，风俗也各不一样。
Customs vary from place to place.

正如刚柔轻重迟速的特性各不相同。
People's temperaments also differ: Some are rough, some are gentle; some are impulsive, some are cautious; some are quick, some are slow.

五味也各有所异，使用的器械也各有不同。
The five flavors are different and implements used by people are different.

衣服的材料和样式也各有不同。
The materials and patterns of clothing are different.

施以礼仪教育，不改变其生活习俗。
Educate the people about the etiquette but do not change their customs.

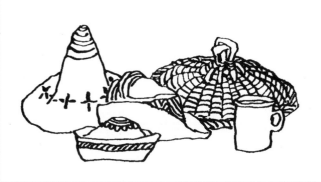

统一其公共设施，不妨碍其生活的便利。
Use uniform public facilities without causing any inconvenience to people's lives.

司寇正刑明辟，以听狱讼。必三刺。有旨无简不听。附从轻，赦从重。凡制五刑，必即天论。邮罚丽于事。

司寇负责审定刑律，明断罪罚，受理一切刑事诉讼。
The Minister of Justice is responsible for examining and approving penal codes, making correct judgment on crime and punishment and handling all criminal cases.

断案必须实行三审制度。
The system of three reviews must be adopted in judging cases.

如果看似有罪，而律无明文规定者，则不起诉。
When someone seems to have committed a crime but the penal code does not have specific provisions regarding this crime, the man will not be prosecuted.

引用律文必取其罚轻者。
When articles of the penal code are cited, the lighter punishment is chosen.

回家喽！
I'm free to go now.

如要赦免，则取其罚重者。
Pardon those who have served long prison sentences.

凡是制定五刑，必须考虑到天伦关系。定罪科罚要有事实依据。
When formulating the five forms of punishment (tattooing the face, cutting off the nose, cutting off the feet, castration and decapitation) the ethical relationships between members of a family must be taken into consideration. We must look at the evidence when convicting somebody of a crime and administering punishment.

析言，破律，乱名，改作，执左道以乱政，杀。作淫声异服，奇技奇器，以疑众，杀。行伪而坚，言伪而辩，学非而博，顺非而泽，以疑众，杀。假于鬼神时日卜筮，以疑众，杀。此四诛者，不以听。

凡割裂文字以曲解法律，混淆概念擅改法律，或挟异端邪道，以罔惑人民、扰乱政治的，当杀！
Those who misinterpret the law, who mix up the concepts and change the meaning of the law, who use heretical beliefs to confuse the people and disturb politics should be executed.

制作靡靡之音、奇装异服、奇技淫巧来动摇民心者，当杀！
Those who create decadent music, outlandish clothes, strange technology or apparatus to sway the mind of the people should be executed.

行为诡诈而使人坚信不渝，言语虚伪而又巧舌如簧，充满邪恶的知识，掩饰罪行以蛊惑民心者，当杀！
Those who persist in performing crafty acts, who are inveterate liars but can speak eloquently, who have a wealth of pernicious knowledge and who conceal their crimes to corrupt people's minds should be executed.

至于假托鬼神之祸福，时日之吉凶，卜筮之休咎，都足以使人惑于见闻，而违悖礼法。当杀！
Those who masquerade as deities and practice divination to predict the future, deliberately causing confusions and puzzlement among the people and making them do things against the rites should be executed.

因为它有悖于国家和民族的根本利益。
Because it is against the fundamental interests of the state and the people.

后天午时三刻……
The day after tomorrow at noon....

这四者属于杀无赦，都不必审理。
Such people can be executed without a public trial.

少而无父者谓之
孤，老而无子
者谓之独，老而
无妻者谓之矜，老而
老而无夫者
谓之寡。
此四者，
天民之穷
而无告者也，皆
有常饩。瘖、聋、
跛、躃、断者、
侏儒、百工，
各以其器食之。

年幼失去父亲的人称为孤。
Gu is used to refer to a child whose father has died.

年老没有子女的人称为独。
Du is used to refer to elderly people with no children.

老年而无妻室的人称作矜。
Guan is used to refer to an old man who has no wife.

老年没有丈夫的人称为寡。
Gua is used to refer to an old woman who has no husband.

礼记图典

45

以上四种人，是世上窘迫而得不到安慰的人，应经常用粮物来接济他们。

These four types of people live in unfortunate circumstances without anyone to give them sympathy. So it is necessary to provide them with food and other necessities on a regular basis.

至于不能说话的，不能听闻的，瘸腿的，不能走路的，肢体不全和身躯矮小的，及一些低等工匠，则应当依其所能而收容和养活他们。

As for the mute and deaf, lame people, crippled people, dwarfs and lowly craftsmen, we should give them a chance to do whatever work they can and provide for them.

我终于可以自食其力了！
Finally I can support myself.

虽然听不见，可我有技术。
Although I cannot hear, I have skills.

礼 运

　　礼运，顾名思义，是讲礼乐的兴衰因革和阴阳造化的流通之理。其中既有对"天下为公"之"大同"理想蓝图的生动描述，又针对"天下为家"的"小康主治"作了具体的规划，并通过上古人类由橧巢营窟演变为宫室台榭生活的历史进程，揭示了"礼"的起源、内容和意义。其间时有警句，精辟而深刻。

The Rise, Evolvement and Decline of *Rites*

This part talks about the rise and decline and the evolvement of rites. It also talks about the rules governing the functions of things in the universe. It gives a vivid description of an ideal world — a world for all. It also has specific plans for what a well-off society should look like. By examining the historical process of people living in caves and then settling down in palaces and houses, it reveals the origin, content and meaning of rites. It is often interspersed with epigrams that are succinct and profound.

礼运

昔者仲尼与于蜡宾，事毕，出游于观之上，喟然而叹。仲尼之叹，盖叹鲁也。言偃在侧曰：「君子何叹？」孔子曰：「大道之行也，与三代之英，丘未之逮也，而有志焉」。

从前，孔子曾被邀请参加蜡祭，充任来宾。事毕，他登上高高的门阙(门两旁的楼)，不觉喟然长叹。孔子之叹，是在叹息鲁国，当时他的弟子言偃陪侍在旁。

Confucius was once invited to take part in a sacrificial offering. After the ceremony was over, Confucius climbed to a high tower by the gate and heaved a deep sigh. He was worried about his home country — the State of Lu. At that time his disciple Yanyan was accompanying him.

大道之行也，天下为公。选贤与能，讲信修睦，故人不独亲其亲，不独子其子。使老有所终，壮有所用，幼有所长，矜、寡、孤独、废疾者，皆有所养。男有分，女有归。

大道通行的时代，天下为天下之人所共有，选举拥戴品德好、能力强的人担任领导，讲究信实，修致和睦。

When the Great Way was prevailing, China was everyone's China. People elected honorable and capable men to be rulers. There was trust and harmony everywhere.

所以人们不仅仅以自己的父母为父母，
People not only considered their own parents as parents;

不仅仅以自己的子女为子女。
They also treated other people's children as their own children.

劳驾了！
Thank you so much.

是这位先生送我回来的！
This gentleman sent me back.

使所有老人得以安度晚年，成人能发挥所长，儿童得到抚育成长。
All old people could spend their remaining years in happiness. Adults could play their roles while children were nurtured.

鳏寡、孤独、伤残者能够受到照顾。
Widowers, widows, orphans and the childless were provided for.

男人各尽其用。
Men could play their part.

女子全有家庭。
Women had their families.

货恶其弃于地也，
不必藏于已，
力恶其不出于
身也，不必
为已。是
故谋闭
而不兴，
盗窃乱贼
而不作，故外
户而不闭。
是谓大同也。

人们厌恶把物品丢弃于地的行为，但并不是由于想占为已有。
People disliked others discarding their belongings on the ground, although not because they coveted it themselves.

厌恶有力而不肯付出的人，却并非想要他为我所用。
People disliked those who were healthy yet remained idle all day, but not because they wanted these people to work for them.

这就叫做"大同"世界。
This is called a world of Great Harmony.

于是一切阴谋诡计都用不上，巧取豪夺之事也不会发生。
So all the scheming and plotting became useless and acquiring other people's belongings by force or trickery never occurred.

因此各家的大门也不用关闭。
No one need to bolt the doors of their homes.

今大道既隐，天下为家，各亲其亲，各子其子，货力为己。大人世及以为礼，城郭沟池以为固，礼义以为纪，以正君臣，以笃父子，以睦兄弟，以和夫妇，以设制度，以立田里，以贤勇知，以功为己。故谋用是作，而兵由此起。

现在大道已经隐没，天下成为一家一姓的财产，各人只亲爱自己的亲人，只慈爱自己的儿女，财物和劳力都为私人所拥有。

Now the Great Way is a thing of the past. China has become the property of one family. People love only their kin; they show affection for only their sons and daughters. Properties and companies are now privately owned.

诸侯们的权力变为世袭的而成为体制，建筑城郭沟池来做为坚固的防守。

The power of dukes and princes has become hereditary, which is part of the established system. Cities are set up with fortifications for defense.

制定礼仪做为纲纪，用来确定君臣的名分，强调父子的慈孝，加深兄弟的和睦，调和夫妇的感情。

Rite is formulated to guide people's behaviors. Under the rite the social status of the monarch and ministers is clearly defined; emphasis is put on a father being kind and sons being filial. The rite also promotes harmony between brothers and improves the relationship between wife and husband.

设立制度，划分疆界田亩、籍贯人口，看重勇者与智士，把功绩归个人所有。

An administrative system is established. Boundaries are created and land is distributed. People with valor and wisdom are highly regarded. Merits belong to individuals.

因此，欺诈巧取的奸谋就跟着发生，而战争也由此出现。

However, machinations and plotting occurred and were followed by wars.

禹、汤、文、武、成王、周公，由此其选也。此六君子者，未有不谨于礼者也，以著其义，以考其信，著有过，刑仁讲让，示民有常。如有不由此者，在执者去，众以为殃，是为小康。

禹、汤、文、武、成王、周公，便因此成为最优秀的人物。这六位君王，没有不恪守礼制的。
Yu, Tang, King Wen, King Wu, King Cheng and Lord Zhou become great leaders. These six Kings all strictly observed the rites.

禮
Rite

大禹
Yu

商汤
Tang

文王
King Wen

成王 King Cheng

Lord Zhou 周公

并以此来发挥其宗旨，考验其信实，指明错误，取法仁爱，讲求逊让之道，昭示人民以行为的常法。
Under such leaders the rite served its purpose. It tested people's trust, pointed out their mistakes and required them to show their benevolence and modesty. In a word, it demonstrated to people what proper social behavior was.

如有越轨或反常的行为，即使是在位的君主，也必斥逐。
If someone deviated from the right course and did something perverse, even if this man was a king, he would be reprimanded and expelled.

并使大家知道，他是罪魁祸首。
Tell everyone that he is the chief culprit.

言偃復問曰：如此乎禮之急也？孔子曰：夫禮，先王以承天之道，以治人之情，故失之者死，得之者生。《詩》曰：「相鼠有體，人而無禮；人而無禮，胡不遄死！」

言偃又问道："礼真是这样重要吗？"孔子说："礼本来是先王秉承自然的法则，来约束人的行为的。所以失去它便不能生存，得到它才不至消亡。"
Yanyan asked, "Do we need rite so urgently?" Confucius answered, "Rite is the natural laws and principles followed by our former kings and used to restrain people's behavior. Without it we cannot exist. With it we won't head for destruction."

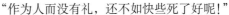

"《诗》中说：'老鼠还有个形体，人类怎能没有礼？'"
The Book of Songs says, "Even the mouse has a body. How can mankind live without rite?"

"作为人而没有礼，还不如快些死了好呢！"
"A man who does not know a thing about rite is no better than a dead person."

是故夫礼，必本于天，殽于地，列于鬼神，达于丧、祭、射、御、冠、昏、朝、聘。故圣人以礼示之，故天下国家可得正也。

因此礼要根据天，效仿地，配合鬼神，而表现在丧、祭、射、御、婚、冠、朝、聘等礼仪上。

So rite should be formulated in line with the rules governing heaven and earth and in support of gods. It shall be demonstrated at the rituals for funerals, sacrificial offerings, archery, driving, marriage, coming-of-age parties, and audiences with the emperor.

圣人正是用这些礼仪来提示正道和人情，而使天下国家有条不紊的呀！

The saints use these rituals to show people the right course and relationships between people so that everything in the country is in proper order.

言偃复问曰：夫子之极言礼也，可得而闻与？孔子曰：我欲观夏道，是故之杞而不足征也，吾得《夏时》焉。我欲观殷道，是故之宋而不足征也，吾得《坤乾》焉。《坤乾》之义，《夏时》之等，吾以是观之。

言偃又问："老师认为礼是这样重要，是否可以给我们讲一讲？"孔子说："我曾想观摩夏代的礼制，因此到夏之后的杞国去考察，但连证据都没留下来。我在那里得到《夏时》一书。"

Yanyan asked again, "Since you consider rite so important, can you elaborate on it?" Confucius said, "Once I desired to learn something about the system of rite of the Xia Dynasty. So I went on an inspection tour to the State of Qi, where the descendants of the Xia live. But the evidence has all been destroyed or lost. The only thing I got is the book *Farming Season of the Xia*."

"我又想看一看殷代的仪礼，因而到殷之后的宋国去考察，但证据几乎都不存在了，我得到了《乾坤》一书。"

"Then I wanted to know the system of rite of the Yin Dynasty. I went on an inspection tour to the State of Song, where the descendants of the Yin live. Evidence did not exist there, either. I got the book *Heaven and Earth*."

"我是根据《坤乾》中的阴阳作用，和《夏时》这一历书的节次来考证的。"

"I studied the rite of the yin (cold) based on the functions of yin and yang (heat) discussed in *Heaven and Earth* and the rite of the Xia based on the farming seasons talked about in *Farming Season of the Xia*."

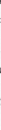

《夏时》当为《夏小正》，是一部有关农时的历书。

I am almost certain that *Farming Season of the Xia* is the same book that called *Xia Xiaozheng*.

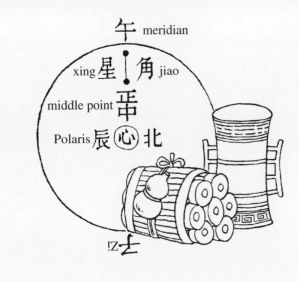

《乾坤》当为商易之《归藏》，其义理与《周易》相类。

Heaven and Earth is also called *Guizang*. The ideas and principles it talks about are similar to those in *The Book of Changes*.

夫礼之初，始诸饮食，其燔黍捭豚，污尊而抔饮，蒉桴而土鼓，犹若可以致其敬于鬼神。及其死也，升屋而号，告曰：皋某复！然后饭腥而苴孰。故天望而地藏也，体魄则降，知气在上。故死者北首，生者南乡，皆从其初。

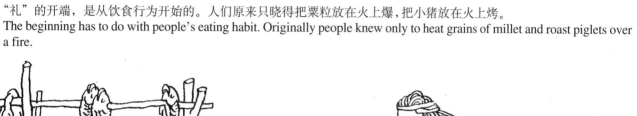

"礼"的开端，是从饮食行为开始的。人们原来只晓得把粟粒放在火上爆，把小猪放在火上烤。
The beginning has to do with people's eating habit. Originally people knew only to heat grains of millet and roast piglets over a fire.

挖地成洼，用作容器，以手捧着喝水。
They dug hollows in the ground as receptacles for water. They scooped up water with their hands and drank it.

删草扎成鼓槌，筑地为鼓。他们以为这样一来就算是向祖先和天地致其敬意了。
They bundled up wool grass as drumsticks and beat the ground as a way of paying tribute to their ancestors, as well as heaven and earth.

到了他们死的时侯，生者便登上屋顶，向天穹呼叫。
When someone died, people would climb to the top of a house and shout to the sky.

然后就用生的谷类放在死者的口里，用草叶包着熟食一起入葬。
They put uncooked grain in the dead person's mouth. Then he or she would be buried in the ground along with some cooked food wrapped in grass leaves.

啊呀，亲人呀，你回来吧！
Come back, my beloved one.

古人所以这样招魂，是由于他们以为在地下的死者，肉体是降入地下了，灵魂却仍在天上。
In this way ancient people used to call back the spirit of the dead. They believed that when someone died, his body went to the ground but his spirit was up in the sky.

因此后世的死者入葬时头向北，而活人则以南向为尊，这些都是从那个年代传下来的。
Later when people died they would be buried with their head facing north. But for people who are alive to sit facing south was a way of showing their high social status. This practice was passed down from ancient times.

昔者先王未有宫室，冬则居营窟，夏则居橧巢。未有火化，食草木之实鸟兽之肉，饮其血茹其毛。未有麻丝，衣其羽皮。后圣有作，然后修火之利，范金合土，以为台榭宫室牖户。以炮，以燔，以亨，以炙，以为醴酪。治其麻丝，以为布帛。以养生送死，以事鬼神上帝，皆从其朔。

从前先王没有宫殿房屋。冬天就住在土窟里，夏天则住在薪柴所搭的窝巢中。
Our former kings did not live in the imperial palaces. They lived in cave dwellings in winter and simple huts made from wood blocks in summer.

不会用火来去除腥气，吃草木的果实，鸟兽的肉。
They didn't know to use fire to get the damp out. They ate the fruits of trees and grass and the meat of birds and animals.

吸饮鸟兽鲜血，带毛生吞。没有丝麻，只穿鸟羽和兽皮。
They drank the blood of birds and animals and ate the raw meat. Since there was no silk or flax, they made clothes from bird's feathers and animal's hide.

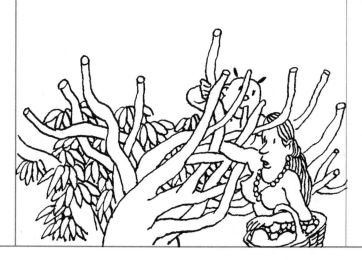

圣人出现后，就开始利用火的功能，加工金属，烧制陶器。
After the saint emerged, he told the people about the many functions of fire. He led them in smelting metal and making pottery from clay.

然后用来建筑台榭、宫殿、屋室、门窗。
Then these materials were used to construct towers, pavilions, palaces, houses as well as doors and windows.

用火来烙和烤，煮和炙，酿制醋酒和乳酪。
They stewed and roasted food over a fire and made wine and cheese.

也用它处理麻丝，而织成麻布和丝绸，用来供给人们生活和料理后事。
They used fire to process raw flax and silk and weave them into cloth to be used in daily life and for funerals.

以及用来祭祀鬼神和上帝，这都是从那时开始的。
Fire was also used when people made sacrificial offerings to the spirits and gods.

故玄酒在室，醴盏在户，粱醍在堂，澄酒在下，陈其牺牲，备其鼎俎，列其琴瑟管磬钟鼓，修其祝嘏，以降上神与其先祖，以正君臣，以笃父子，以睦兄弟，以齐上下，夫妇有所，是谓承天之祜。

……祝以孝告，嘏以慈告，是谓大祥。

此礼之大成也。

所以在祭祀时，玄酒反而在室，醴和盏在户，斋醍在堂，澄酒居堂下。

In a sacrificial offering ritual, xuanjiu is placed in the main room, li and zan near the gate, ziti in the lobby and chengjiu outside the lobby.

以上五种祭酒，各依等级而设，玄酒即泉水，为远古无酒时所用，是因尊古而称之，设于室内靠北边；醴，一种甜酒；盏，一种葱白色的酒，因是后世所为，所以虽在室内，而稍南近户；粱醍，一种红赤色的酒，又低一等，列于堂上；澄酒，即有沉滓的酒，列于堂下。

The above five types of liquid are ranked in descending order. Xuanjiu, or spring water, was used in antiquity when there was no wine. It is placed inside the main room near the northern side. Li, a type of sweet wine, and zan, a white-colored wine are placed inside the main room to the southern side near the gate. Ziti, a red-colored wine, is placed in the lobby. Chengjiu, a type of wine with dregs, is placed just outside the lobby.

然后陈列供祭的牺牲，备齐祭器，安排琴瑟管磬钟鼓。准备好主人告神之辞(祝)，和象征神的"尸"致福于主人之辞(嘏)，用以迎接上神和先祖的降临。

Then slaughtered animals used as sacrifice are set out together with the sacrificial vessels as well as zithers, pipes, chime stones, bells and drums. They have already written the host's message to god and a message conveying god's blessings to the host. Now they are ready to greet the descent of gods and ancestors.

辨正君臣之义，增厚父子的感情，和睦兄弟的情谊，主人主妇各尽职守，即可称为承受了上天的福祉。

When a monarch and his ministers know their appropriate actions, when the relationship between a father and son is improved, when friendship between brothers is promoted and when the host and his wife each performs his/her duty diligently, then we can say that they are blessed by god.

Representative of one's ancestors or god

受祭者尸

祝辞上充满后辈的敬畏。嘏辞上体现着祖先的慈爱，这就算是大吉大祥，是"礼"最圆满的结果了。
The host's message is full of sentences showing descendants' awe and respect. The message from heaven shows the affection and kindness of their forefathers. This is considered auspicious and the most satisfactory result of the rite.

Person presiding over the sacrificial offering ritual

主祭者

礼记图典

66

孔子曰：呜呼哀哉！我观周道，幽厉伤之。吾舍鲁何适矣！鲁之郊禘，非礼也，周公其衰矣！杞之郊也，禹也。宋之郊也，契也。是天子之事守也。故天子祭天地，诸侯祭社稷。

孔子说："唉，真是太可悲了！我考察周代的制度，自幽王、厉王起就已把周礼破坏了，除了鲁国，我到哪里去呢？"
Confucius said, "This is sad. I have studied the Zhou Dynasty system. I found that rite of the Zhou was undermined in King You and King Li's time. Where can I go except the State of Lu?"

但鲁国举行的郊天之祭却是不合于礼的。周公的礼制已经衰微了啊！
But the sacrificial offering ritual performed by the State of Lu to a god does not conform to the requirement of rite. The system of rite of the Lord of Zhou exists no longer.

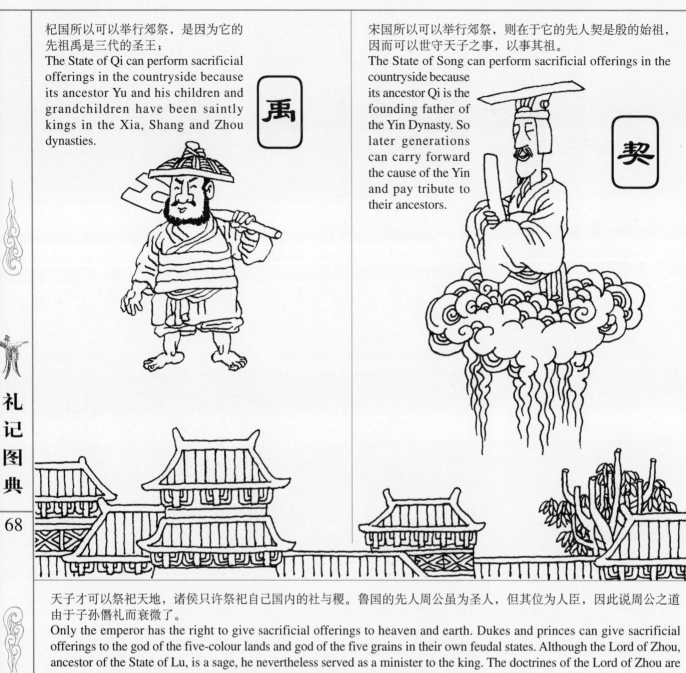

杞国所以可以举行郊祭，是因为它的先祖禹是三代的圣王；
The State of Qi can perform sacrificial offerings in the countryside because its ancestor Yu and his children and grandchildren have been saintly kings in the Xia, Shang and Zhou dynasties.

禹

宋国所以可以举行郊祭，则在于它的先人契是殷的始祖，因而可以世守天子之事，以事其祖。
The State of Song can perform sacrificial offerings in the countryside because its ancestor Qi is the founding father of the Yin Dynasty. So later generations can carry forward the cause of the Yin and pay tribute to their ancestors.

契

天子才可以祭祀天地，诸侯只许祭祀自己国内的社与稷。鲁国的先人周公虽为圣人，但其位为人臣，因此说周公之道由于子孙僭礼而衰微了。
Only the emperor has the right to give sacrificial offerings to heaven and earth. Dukes and princes can give sacrificial offerings to the god of the five-colour lands and god of the five grains in their own feudal states. Although the Lord of Zhou, ancestor of the State of Lu, is a sage, he nevertheless served as a minister to the king. The doctrines of the Lord of Zhou are neglected by his descendants who have violated the rite.

是故礼者，君之大柄也。所以别嫌明微，傧鬼神，考制度，别仁义，所以治政安君也。故政不正，则君位危；君位危，则大臣倍，小臣窃。刑肃而俗敝，则法无常；法无常，而礼无列；礼无列，则士不事也。刑肃而俗敝，则民弗归也，是谓疵国。

所以说"礼"，是君主执以治国的把柄。因为有了它才能判别是非，洞察幽隐。

Kings depend on the rite to govern their countries. Without rite, we cannot distinguish right from wrong, or see clearly what is not easily discernable.

才能接待神祇。才可划分等级，规定章法。

Without rite, we cannot approach god, or define social classes, or formulate laws and regulations.

才可建立伦常，区别尊亲。

Without rite, we cannot establish ethical relationships among people or determine whom one should respect and stay close to.

"礼"是用来处理政事和巩固君权的。所以政事施行不得其法，君位就会发生动摇。君位动摇，大臣们便不听指挥，小臣们则乘机营私。

Rite is used as a tool in the administration of a government to consolidate the emperor's power. So if the government does not know the proper way to administer a country, the emperor's authority would be jeopardized. As a result, the senior ministers would not follow orders and petty officials would take the chance to seek private gains.

尽管有严刑峻罚取缔这些敝端，却形成了寡廉鲜耻的风气，而法令又时时更变，法令时时更变，礼节便也随之纷乱。

The rulers would resort to draconian laws and punishment to remove such malpractice, but the shameless atmosphere would have already been well established. What's more, the rulers make constant changes to the laws and regulations, causing confusion to the rite.

礼节纷乱，则士人将手足无措。刑罚严急，风气败坏，则人民就离心离德了。

The confusion to the rite would puzzle officials and scholars. Harsh punishment and widespread malpractice would cause dissension and discord among the people.

这样的国家可以叫病疵之国了。

A country such as this is heading for serious trouble.

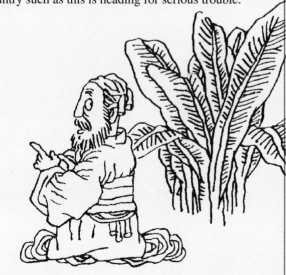

故政者，君之所以藏身也，是故夫政本于天，殽以降命。命降于社之谓殽地，降于祖庙之谓仁义，降于山川之谓兴作，降于五祀之谓制度。此圣人所以藏身之固也。

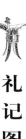

政治行为是一国之君的托身之所在，所以人君之政必本于天而效法之，以布命天下。
Political activities are essential to a king. So a king's political program must follow the rules of heaven before he rules his country.

因祭社而出命，是效地之政(效其高下之势，以定尊卑)。
After giving sacrificial offerings to the god of the five-colour lands, the king formulates rules to govern the behavior of people of different social strata (as there are upper classes and lower classes).

有事于祖庙而出命，是仁义之政(亲亲为仁；尊尊为义)。
After giving sacrificial offerings to the ancestors, the king formulates policies related to benevolence and loyalty.

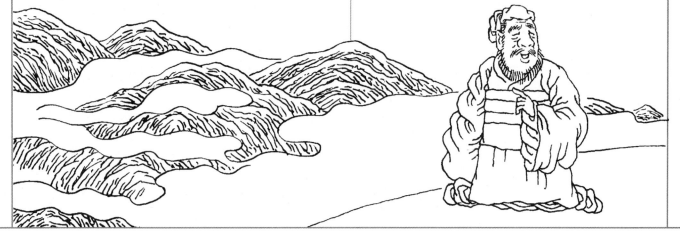

有事于山川而出命，是兴作之政（是为建设）。
After giving sacrificial offerings to the gods of mountains and rivers, the king formulates policies regarding construction.

有事于五祀而出命，是制度之政（是为将自然的精神制度化）。
After giving sacrificial offerings to the five elements of the physical world (metal, wood, water, fire, earth), the king formulates rules on the system of governance.

五行配五常图
Combination of the five elements and the five constant virtues

通过这样的政治行为，圣人就可以安身保国了。
These political activities will further strengthen the position of the sage.

这不是都成老百姓了吗？
Isn't everybody an ordinary person now?

故圣人参于天地，并于鬼神，以治政也；处其所存，礼之序也；玩其所乐，民之治也。故天生时而地生财，父生而师教之，四者君以正用之，故君者立于无过之地也。

因此圣人合同天地而为三，与鬼神并立而为两，以此管理众人之事。

The sage would work with the heaven, the earth and all the gods to administer public affairs.

归纳其体察的结果，则是礼的秩序。

The result of his observation of heaven, earth and all gods is an order created on the basis of rite.

顺应自然的法则，则人民也就得到了恰当的安置。

By following nature's laws and rules, people will find their appropriate places.

人由父母所生，而由老师教授知识。这四者，做君主的要运用得当。

The life of a person is given by his/her parents. He gains knowledge from a teacher. A monarch should handle these four types of people in an appropriate manner.

这样君主就立于最恰当的位置上了。

By doing so the monarch would find himself in the most suited position.

所以四时生于天，百货产于地。

The four seasons are created by heaven and a myriad of products grown on earth.

以上是讲人君应正身修德，顺天之时，因地之利，而裁成其道，辅相其宜，以使百姓养生丧死而无憾的道理。也即"礼"的产生与作用。

The above talks about how a monarch should be a man of integrity. He should go with the timing of heaven and take advantage of the earth's products and formulate a system so that ordinary people can lead a life without regrets from birth to death. This is closely related to the creation and functioning of the rite.

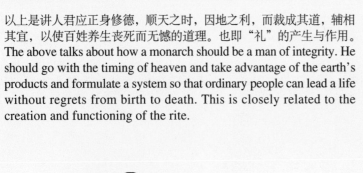

故圣人耐以天下为
一家，以中国
为一人者，必
知其情，
辟于其义，
明于其
利，达
于其患；
然后
能为之。
何谓人情？
喜、怒、哀、
惧、爱、恶、欲，
七者弗学而能。
非意之也，

所以圣人能把天下当作一家，把天下人视为同自己一样，并不是一厢情愿。
A sage would consider all people on earth as one big family and think of all other people as he would himself.

他必须做到了解人情，通晓义理，明白利害之所在，清楚人的忧患，才能做到这一点。
He must understand people's feelings and the truth behind these feelings. He must know what is beneficial and what is harmful to them. He must also understand their worries and fears.

什么是人情呢？人情就是喜、怒、哀、惧、爱、恶、欲。这七种心理因素，不必学习，就能做到。
What are people's feelings comprised of ? They are joy, anger, sorrow, fear, love, hatred and desire. These feelings are not learnt.

何谓人义？父慈，子孝，兄良，弟弟，夫义，妇听，长惠，幼顺，君仁，臣忠，十者谓之人义。讲信修睦，谓之人义。争夺相杀，谓之人患。故圣人之所以治人七情，修十义，讲信修睦，尚辞让，去争夺，舍礼何以治之？

什么是人义？人义就是为父须慈，为子须孝，为兄须良，为弟须悌，
What is human righteousness? It means a father should be kind, a son should be filial; an elder brother should love his younger brother who in turn should show respect for his elder brother.

为夫须义，为妇须服从，
A husband must be honorable; a wife must be submissive.

为长者须体恤下情，为幼者须虚心受教，
An elderly person should show concern for the young; a young person must listen to an elderly person's advice with an open mind.

为君须仁，为臣者须忠。这十项标准，就是人义。
Monarchs should be benevolent and ministers should be loyal. These ten criteria constitute what we call human righteousness.

彼此讲究信用，维护和睦，这就叫做"人利"。
Everyone keeps his word and maintains harmonious relationships with others; this is called "human benefit."

彼此争夺相残，这就叫做"人患"。
People fighting and harming each other just to scramble for something is called "human scourge."

亦是君子之为君子的准则。
This is what a gentleman is supposed to do. It is also the measure of a gentleman.

所以圣人要协调人们的七情，建立十项标准，讲究信用，维护和睦，崇尚辞让，摒弃争夺。能做到这一点，除了礼教，还有什么更好的方法呢？
So a sage will coordinate the seven feelings of man and establish the ten criteria. He will get everyone to keep his word, maintain harmony, advocate modesty and relinquish fighting. What better way to achieve this purpose than rite?

饮食男女，人之大欲存焉。死亡贫苦，人之大恶存焉。故欲恶者，心之大端也。人藏其心，不可测度也。美恶皆在其心，不见其色也，欲一以穷之，舍礼何以哉？

饮食、男女之事，是人类最基本的需求。
Eating and love between a man and woman are the most fundamental needs of human beings.

死亡与贫苦，又是人类最害怕的事情。
Death and poverty are the two things people fear most.

这两种好恶，是人心理上两大最强烈的意志。
These two types of likes and dislikes are the most powerful sentiments in a person's mind.

但人们却惯于隐藏自己的意图，使大家无从识别测度。
But people are good at concealing their intentions so that others will have no idea about them.

爱好和嫌恶都隐藏在心里，而不表现在外貌上。
Likes and dislikes are buried deep down rather than shown on their face.

藏在心里是块病。
Holding it back will make you sick.

人的七情好恶，以十义为标准，则举止自然合礼；若七情乖僻，有悖人伦，则他的言行中也会表露无遗。
When a person's seven feelings (including his likes and dislikes) follow the ten criteria of righteousness, he will bear himself in the most natural way in conformity with rite. If a person's seven feelings are oppressed, they will nevertheless be shown in his acts or speech.

若要使其整个暴露出来，除了用礼还有什么更好的方法呢？
What better way to bring the sentiments out than rite?

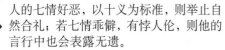

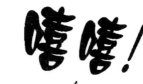

故人者，其天地之德，阴阳之交，鬼神之会，五行之秀气也。故天秉阳，垂日星，地秉阴，窍于山川，播五行于四时，和而后月生也。是以三五而盈，三五而阙。五行之动，迭相竭也。五行四时十二月，还相为本也。

所以人，就是天地的德性，阴阳两性的交合，鬼神相会，五种元素的最佳组合而产生的呀！
So man is the product created when heaven and earth, yin (cold) and yang (heat) join together, when spirits come into contact with each other and when the five elements are combined in the best way.

天由于属阳，得以产生出光辉的日月星辰。
In nature, heaven is yang. It produced the sun, the moon and all the stars that shine.

地由于属阴，所以山河得以充满生气。
In nature, earth is yin. So rivers and mountains are full of vitality.

把木火金水分配在大地上为四时，节气均匀，十二月就产生了。
When the four elements — wood, fire, metal, water — are spread on earth, they become the four seasons with 24 seasonal division points distributed evenly in between. Thus the 12 months come into existence.

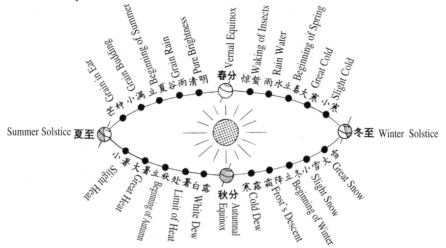

每月前十五天，月亮由残缺而趋圆满。
In the first 15 days of each month, the moon's size and brightness gradually increase until the moon is full.

后十五日又由圆满渐趋残缺。
In the last 15 days of each month, the moon gradually decreases in size and brightness once again.

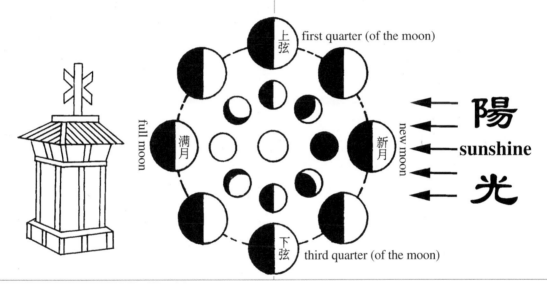

五行的周而复始，过去的终结成为后来的开始，如环无端。
The five elements move perpetually in cycles, the end of the past becoming the beginning of the future like a loop without an end.

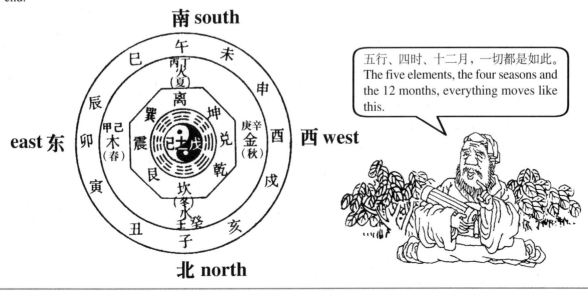

五行、四时、十二月，一切都是如此。
The five elements, the four seasons and the 12 months, everything moves like this.

以天地为本，故物可举也；以阴阳为端，故情可睹也；以四时为柄，故事可劝也；以日星为纪，故事可列也，月以为量，故功有艺也；鬼神以为徒，故事可守也；五行以为质，故事可复也；礼义以为器，故事行有考也；人情以为田，故人以为奥也；四灵以为畜，故饮食有由也。

以天地为根本，所以能涵盖万物。
When heaven and earth are considered to be of basic importance, everything else is included.

以阴阳为大端，可以由此及彼地对事物进行观察。
Guided by the principle of yin (cold) and yang (heat), we can observe things that are opposites.

以四时为依据，可以提醒人们不要忘记农时。
The four seasons remind people of the right time for farming.

以日星为准则，可以使事情条理分明。
With the sun and stars as the natural law, everything is placed in good order.

以月为量，可以使工作有时限。
One can set a time limit for his work according to the moon.

以鬼神为伴侣，会使人忠于职守。
With the gods for company, man can perform his duties diligently.

以五行为原理，会使工作有始有终。
Based on the principles of the five elements, people will carry their work through to the end.

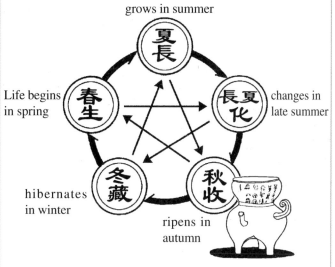

以礼义为约束，可以使行为有规范。
Rite and righteousness can keep people's actions within the bounds of the norm of society.

以人性为对象，可以打动人的心灵。
You can move a person by targeting his feelings.

以四灵为家畜，可以使饮食有来源。
Breed the four wise animals as livestock and one will have a source of food.

故礼义也者，人之大端也。所以讲信修睦，而固人肌肤之会，筋骸之束也。所以养生、送死、事鬼神之大端也，所以达天道、顺人情之大窦也。故唯圣人为知礼之不可以已也。故坏国、丧家、亡人，必先去其礼。故礼之于人也，犹酒之有糵也，君子以厚，小人以薄。

所谓礼义，是人之所以为人的最基本的特征。
Rite and righteousness are the underlying characteristics of a human being.

人有礼义然后才能讲究信义，维护和睦，就像人的肌肤、筋骨连在一起那样。
With rite and righteousness, people will keep their word and maintain harmony, just like the way a person's muscles, skin, tendons and bones are joined.

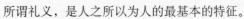

人们靠"礼"来经营生活、料理死者，以"礼"作为供奉神灵的手段，以疏通天道和人情。
People use rite to manage their life and handle the deceased. Rite is a means through which people give sacrificial offerings to the gods so that human feelings conform to the Way of Heaven.

所以只有圣人知道礼是不可废止的。
So only the sage knows that rite should not be abolished.

至于国破家亡，个人身败名裂，则肯定是他们丢掉了"礼"的缘故。
When a country falls and a family is broken, or when a person brings disgrace and ruin upon himself, it is most likely that they have thrown rite away.

因而，礼对于人们，就像酿酒用的酒曲。
Rite to people is like yeast to wine.

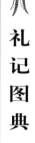

wine

君子像味道醇厚的酒，
A gentleman is like a mellow wine.

小人有如味道薄劣的酒。
A wicked person is like a wine that tastes awful.

故圣王修义之柄，礼之序，以治人情。故人情者，圣王之田也，修礼以耕之，陈义以种之，讲学以耨之，本仁以聚之，播乐以安之。故礼也者，义之实也。协诸义而协，则礼虽先王未之有，可以义起也。

所以先王修明义的根本，"礼"的秩序，用以培育人情。所以人情这一因素，有如圣王所要耕种的土地，用"礼"为工具来耕作它。

So our late king emphasized the importance of righteousness and rite to nurture people's feelings. Our late king, the sage, used rite as the tool to cultivate the land of human feelings.

以义理为种籽来播种。
He sowed the seeds of righteousness.

用学习探讨来保护它。
He protected it and made it grow with learning and discussion.

用仁爱为纽带来联络它。
He used benevolence to link it.

用音乐使人们习惯它。
He used music to get people accustomed to it.

凡是比照义而与之相契合的，即使在先王那里还没有，也完全可以根据义来创造它。
Anything conforming to righteousness, even if it did not exist during the days of our late king, can be created according to righteousness.

義
righteousness

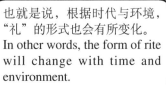

也就是说，根据时代与环境，"礼"的形式也会有所变化。
In other words, the form of rite will change with time and environment.

所以礼，又可以说成是义的果实。
In a sense, rite is the fruit of righteousness.

义者，艺之分，仁之节也。协于艺，讲于仁，得之者强。仁者，义之本也，顺之体也，得之者尊。故治国不以礼，犹无耜而耕也。为礼不本于义，犹耕而弗种也。为义而不讲之以学，犹种而弗耨也。讲之以学而不合之以仁，犹耨而弗获也。合之以仁而不安之以乐，犹获而弗食也。安之以乐而不达于顺，犹食而弗肥也。

义是行事的分寸，仁心的品节。
Righteousness is the proper way to do things. It is the embodiment of benevolence.

处事得体，讲究仁道，能做到这一点便无人与之抗争。
If a person can deal with problems in the most appropriate manner while sticking to the principle of benevolence, he will find no rival in this world.

因为仁是义的根本，是顺达天理人情的具体表现。能如此做，就会受到敬服。
This is because benevolence is the foundation of righteousness. It is an indication that what we do is in line with heavenly truth and human feelings. By doing so, you will be held in high regard.

所以治理国家而不用"礼"，就像没有农具而要种田。
Therefore, governing a country without rite is like cultivating land without farm implements.

制"礼"而不以义为根本，就像耕了田而没有播种。
Formulating rites not based on righteousness is like cultivating land without sowing seeds.

有了义而不阐明于众，就像播了种而不去维护。
Not expounding righteousness to the public is like sowing the seeds but not taking care of them.

阐明其意义而不合于仁爱，就像耨过草而没有收成。
Explaining the meaning of righteousness not in conformity with benevolence is like pulling up the weeds in your field but still getting no harvest.

合于仁爱而没有做到自觉自愿的地步，就像收成了而没有吃到口中。
By doing things in line with the principle of benevolence, but not doing them willingly is like gathering in the crops but being unable to eat them.

做到了自觉自愿而不能成为习惯，则又像吃到了口中而得不到健康。
By voluntarily doing the things in concordance with the principles of benevolence but not being in the habit of doing so is like eating the food but your health not benefiting from it.

倒霉!
Bad luck!

四体既正，肤革充盈，人之肥也。父子笃，兄弟睦，夫妇和，家之肥也。大臣法，小臣廉，官职相序，君臣相正，国之肥也。天子以德为车，以乐为御，诸侯以礼相与，大夫以法相序，士以信相考，百姓以睦相守，天下之肥也。是谓大顺。大顺者，所以养生送死事鬼神之常也。

四体已经正常，皮肤又丰满，就是个健康的身体了。
With fine skin and all four limbs in good condition, a person is in good health.

父子相亲，兄弟和睦，夫妇相爱，即为一个健康的家庭了。
Father and son have cordial relations, brothers live in harmony and husband and wife love each other — such is a healthy family.

大臣们奉公守法，小臣们清正廉洁，行政有序，君臣能互相勉励匡正，就是个正常的国家了。
Senior ministers are law-abiding, minor officials are decent and honest. Administration is in good order. The monarch and his ministers give encouragement and counsel to each other. Such is a normal country.

天子以其德行为车，用言与乐来驾御它。

An emperor's virtue is like a wagon, he controls this wagon with his speech and music.

诸侯间都按"礼"交往。

Dukes and princes interact with each other through rite.

大夫间都以法规相合作。

Officials cooperate with each other in line with laws and regulations.

士与士之间以诚信相往来。

Scholars communicate with other scholars on the basis of trust.

百姓以和睦共同生活。这就是个健康的世界，可称为大顺。大顺就是人们养生送死，顺应自然的道理。

Ordinary people live together in harmony. Such is a healthy world. This we call dashun. It is a condition whereby people alive are provided for and dead people are buried properly — everything they do is in line with the principles governing nature.

故事大积焉而不苑。并行而不谬，细行而不失。深而通，茂而有间，连而不相及也，动而不相害也。此顺之至也。故明于顺，然后能守危也。

因此，虽万事丛叠也不至于郁滞，两事伴行也不至于彼此互错，微末的小事也不至于遗漏。

Even when many things pile up they do not hinder each other. Two things can work side by side without ever affecting the other. Minute matters are not neglected.

深奥的可以弄懂，茂密的可以分开，连接的又不互相牵扯，活动的又不互相戕害。

Esoteric things can be understood; dense things can be separated; things joined together won't affect each other; things on the move won't harm each other.

这才是顺的极致。所以了解顺的意义，然后能居高而不险。

This is the acme of shun. After you understand the meaning of shun, you can stand at a precipitous height without any danger.

故礼之不同也，不丰也，不杀也，所以持情而合危也。故圣王所以顺，山者不使居川，不使渚者居中原，而弗敝也。用水、火、金、木，饮食必时，合男女，颁爵位，必当年德，用民必顺。故无水旱昆虫之灾，民无凶饥妖孽之疾。

祭祀之礼是有不同等级的，应俭者不可丰，应隆者不可少。以此来维护人情，和合上下，不使危乱。

The rite for sacrificial offerings has different rankings. A supposedly spare sacrificial offering shouldn't be abundant while a supposedly abundant sacrificial offering shouldn't be spare. This is a way to maintain human relations and keep harmony between the superior and subordinate so that no danger or chaos will ever occur.

因此圣王顺乎民情，不使居住在山地的人去过河川地带的生活。

To comply with the popular will, the sage king won't force residents living in mountains to lead a life in the river valleys.

也不使居住在河川地带的人移居到中原生活，这才不至于使人们感到生活不便。

Nor will he force people living by the rivers to move to the central plains. He doesn't want to cause any inconvenience to people's life.

使用水、火、金属、木料及饮食都应根据一定的季节和天时。
The use of water, fire, metal, timber and food must be in line with specific seasons and time.

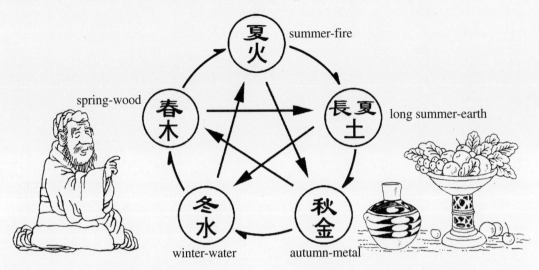

spring-wood
summer-fire
long summer-earth
winter-water
autumn-metal

男女婚配，颁赐爵位，都要与年龄和德行相当。
Marriage between a man and a woman and the granting of titles of nobility should correspond with age and virtue.

用人要顺应天时、地利和人情的条件。
The use of human resources must comply with climate, favorable geographical position and human relations.

如在农闲时，才可用民役。
Only in the off-peak farming season shall peasants be drafted to do construction work.

所以就没有水旱昆虫的灾害，人民就不会有凶饥妖孽的骚扰了。
So people will not suffer from flood, drought, or disaster caused by pests.

凶饥

妖

孽

学　记

学记为儒家论述教学原理的经典文献。记述了古代的教育制度、教学内容和方法，对教学循序渐进的一般过程、教学方法的得失、教师的责任、尊师重道的意义、教者与学者之间的辩证关系等，都作了系统的阐述，并一直为后世所遵循。

On Learning

This is a classical document on the principle of teaching and learning of the Confucian school. It recounts the education system, the content of teaching and teaching method in ancient times. It says that teaching should proceed step by step in an orderly way. It gives a systematic account of teaching methods (discussing the good and bad ones), teachers' responsibilities, the significance of respecting the teacher, and the dialectical relationship between teacher and student. People of later generations consider many of the opinions and methods in the book correct and effective.

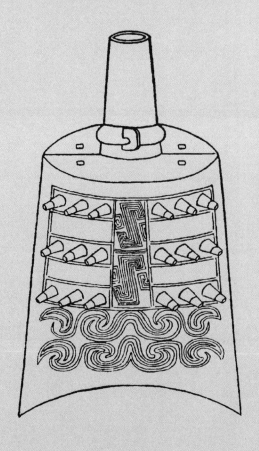

发虑宪，求善良，足以谀闻，不足以动众。就贤体远，足以动众，未足以化民。君子如欲化民成俗，其必由学乎！

发动谋虑，招求善良，足以做到小有声望，但不足以感动众人。

Working out a political program and recruiting virtuous and capable people to work for you can secure you some reputation but it won't be enough to appeal to the general public.

礼贤下士，体察致远，足以感动众人，但不足以教化人民。

Treating your officials well and having a vision for the future will appeal to the general public. But it won't be enough to educate the people.

君子要教化百姓，形成良好的习俗，一定要从教育开始。

For a gentleman to teach the people good manners, he must start with education.

其此之謂乎！

「念終始典于學。」

為先。《兌命》曰：

建國君民，教學

是故古之王者

人不學，不知道。

玉不琢，不成器；

玉的质地虽然美好，但不加琢磨，就不会成为美好的器物。
Although the quality of jade is good, it will not become a beautiful object without carving and polishing.

人虽贵为万物之长，但不通过学习，也不会明白道理。
Although man is the cleverest of all living beings, he will not understand the truth without learning.

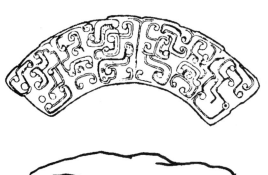

因此古代君王建立国家、治理人民，必以教育为优先的任务。
Therefore all monarchs in ancient time considered education their priority in establishing a country and ruling the people.

《尚书·兑命》中说："从始至终都要想着学习。"就是说的这个意思吧！
The Book of History says, "Onc should think of studying from the beginning to the end."

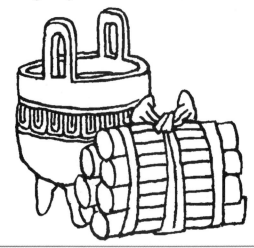

虽有嘉肴，弗食不知其旨也；虽有至道，弗学不知其善也。是故学然后知不足，教然后知困。知不足，然后能自反也；知困，然后能自强也。故曰教学相长也。《兑命》曰：「学学半」。其此之谓乎！

虽有美味的食物，不去品尝，就不知它的滋味。
Delicious food exists; but if you never try it you won't know what it tastes like.

虽有至善的道理，不去学习，就不知它的完美。
There are perfect truths; but if you don't learn them you will never know how wonderful they are.

通过学习，然后才知道自己的不足。教了人家之后才知道自己的不懂之处。

Through learning you will become aware of your weaknesses. Through teaching you will recognize matters you don't understand very well.

知道不足，然后才能自我反省；知道不足，然后才能自我激励。

Realizing your own weaknesses will make you look at yourself introspectively and give yourself encouragement.

所以说，教与学是相辅相成的。
So teaching and learning will complement each other.

《尚书·兑命篇》中说："教和学各是学问的一半。" 说的大概就是这个意思吧！
The Book of History says, "Teaching and learning each is half of scholarship." It means more or less the same thing as what we have just discussed.

大学之教也，时教必有正业，退息必有居学。不学操缦，不能安弦；不学博依，不能安诗；不学杂服，不能安礼；不兴其艺，不能乐学。故君子之于学也，藏焉，修焉，息焉，游焉。

"大学"教育按照时序进行，所教都有恰当的科目。
The education of Great Learning is carried out in the right order, with appropriate subjects taught.

如春秋教以礼乐，冬夏教以诗书，即所谓春诵夏弦之类。
Rite and music are taught in spring and autumn; poetry and *The Book of History* are taught in winter and summer.

学生下课及休假时，要经常温习功课。
Students must revise their lessons after class and during holidays.

不学习操弄琴瑟之弦的基本功，就无法熟练地弹奏乐曲。
If you don't practice the basic skills for playing a zither, you will be unable to play the tunes skillfully.

不能广泛涉猎，就无从将诗做好。
If you don't read extensively, you will be unable to write poetry well.

不学习冕弁之制，就无从行礼。
If you don't learn the etiquette, you will be unable to use it.

不喜欢这些基本功，就提不起学习的乐趣。
If you don't like these basic skills, studying won't be fun for you.

所以君子在学习方面，要藏之于心，反复研究，休息或游玩之间，都不能忘记。
When it comes to learning, a gentleman must research the subject matter again and again, not forgetting it even when he is resting or having fun.

大学之法，禁于未发之谓豫，当其可之谓时，不陵节而施之谓孙，相观而善之谓摩。此四者，教之所由兴也。发然后禁，则扞格而不胜；时过然后学，则勤苦而难成；杂施而不孙，则坏乱而不修；独学而无友，则孤陋而寡闻；燕朋逆其师；燕辟废其学。此六者，教之所由废也。

大学的教人方法，防范过失于未发之前，叫做预防。
A method for educating people by the Great Learning is prevention, or taking precaution so that faults will not materialize.

当学者恰好可以教学时施教，叫做合乎时宜。
Teach a student when he is most ready to learn. This is called appropriate timing.

> 先生，我们有个想法……
> We have an idea, sir.

> 古人曾经这么说……
> A wise man once said...

不超越学者现有的程度而施教，叫做顺序；
Teach a student without exceeding his present level of understanding. This is called order.

使学者互相观摩而得到益处，叫做切磋，这是使教育兴盛的方法。
Let students inspect and learn from each other's work. This method furthers education.

邪念已经萌生，然后加以禁止，则坚不可入，教育亦难有收效。

When an evil idea is brewing, it will be hard to stop it because it is impregnable. Education won't be effective, either.

学习的年龄过去后再学，即使勤奋刻苦，亦难有所获。

Studying when the best age for study has already passed will get you nowhere even if you study hard.

杂乱施教，学习不系统，致使头脑混乱而不可修治。

When teaching is chaotic and learning is not systematic, the student will have an unclear mind beyond correction.

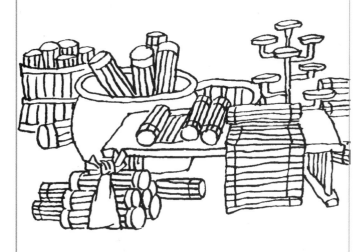

一个人独自学习而没有学友，就会孤单浅薄，见识不广。

If a person studies alone without any fellow students, his knowledge won't be profound or extensive.

结交不正当的朋友，会违背师长的教导。

You will go against your teacher's instructions when you make friends with people of dubious character.

不良的习惯，会荒废个人的学业。

Bad habits will cause you to neglect and fail your studies.

这六项是教育失败的原因。
The above six points are the reasons of failure in education.

君子既知教之所由兴，又知教之所由废，然后可以为人师也。故君子之教喻也，道而弗牵，强而弗抑，开而弗达。道而弗牵则和，强而弗抑则易，开而弗达则思。和、易以思，可谓善喻矣。

君子既知道了教育兴起的原因，又知道了教育衰落的原因，然后可以为人师表。
When a gentleman knows the reasons behind the flourishing or failure of education, he will be able to become a teacher.

所以君子的教育是晓喻别人，只加以引导，而不强迫人服从；
A gentleman's instruction is to enlighten others. He should give them guidance but should not force them to obey.

对学生严格，但不应抑制其个性的发展。
He should be strict with his students but should not oppress the development of their individuality.

加以启发，而不将结论和盘托出。
When explaining the principles of things, a teacher should inspire students by giving them examples instead of arriving at the final conclusion directly.

只引导不强迫，使学习的人感到亲切。
He should guide the students but not force them to learn. In this way the students will think him a kind person.

严格而不抑制，使学生能够自由发展。
Be strict but not oppressive. Give students the freedom to develop their individuality.

只启发而不告之结论，使学生能够勤于思考。
Inspire the students instead of giving them the answer straight away in order to make them think for themselves.

使人亲近和顺理发挥，又能主动思考。
A teacher should always be ready to help the students, inspire them and make them think hard.

完全正确！
Absolutcly right.

这就可以说是善于晓喻了。
A teacher of this sort knows how to enlighten students.

学者有四失，教者必知
之。人之学也或失
则多，或失则寡，或
失则易，或失则止。
此四者，心之莫同也。
知其心，然后
能救其失也。
教也者，
长善而救
其失者也。善歌
者，使人继其声；善
教者，使人继其志。其
言也约而达，微而藏，
罕譬而喻，可谓继志矣。

学生有四种过失，教师一定要知道。
A teacher must know four defects of the students.

多寡易止

人的学习或者失之贪多；或者失之过少；
Some students aspire to learn too much. Other students do not want to learn at all.

或者失之于见异思迁；或者失之于浅尝辄止。
Some students keep shifting their focus to new things. Other students are satisfied with just a little knowledge of a subject.

这四种情况心理状态是不同的，先了解这些心理，然后才能纠正它。
These are four different mental conditions. They need to be identified before they can be corrected.

还是那山高！
That mountain is higher.

教育的目的，是为了提高成绩，而纠正过失。
The purpose of education is to improve performance and correct mistakes.

善于教学的人，能使人继承他的志向。
A person good at teaching can make other people carry on his ambitions.

善于歌唱的人，能把他的演唱技法传给他人。
A person good at singing can pass on his singing skill to others.

他的言辞简约而通达，含蓄而精美，善用譬喻而生动明了。这样就可算是能使人继承志向了。
His words are concise and to the point, implicit and elegant, vivid and easy to understand. He is also good at using metaphors.

凡学之道，严师为难。师严然后道尊，道尊然后民知敬学。是故君之所不臣于其臣者二：当其为尸，则弗臣也；当其为师，则弗臣也。大学之礼，虽诏于天子无北面，所以尊师也。

礼记图典

108

为学之道，一般以尊敬师长最难做到。教师受到尊重，然后真理才能受到尊重。
It's not easy for a student to acknowledge respect for his teacher. But only when teachers are respected will truths be respected.

真理受到尊重，然后百姓才能懂得敬重学业。
When truths are respected, ordinary people will then know the importance of education.

所以君主不以对待下属的态度对待臣子的情况有两种。一种是在祭祀中，臣子做"尸"(神灵的象征者)的时候；
There are two cases when a monarch will not treat his minister as a subordinate: First, when the minister acts as a shi (symbol of god) in a sacrificial offering ritual.

另一种是做君主的老师的时候。大学之"礼"中，为天子授课，臣下不必面北而对。
The second case is when a minister serves as a monarch's teacher. According to the etiquette of the Great Learning, when a minister gives a lesson to his monarch, he doesn't need to sit facing the north.

先生请随意。
Suit yourself.

臣不敢。
I don't dare.

面南为尊者之位，不必面北即不必居臣位。
People of higher ranking always sit facing south. A minister is supposed to face north when he is with the monarch.

这是为了表示对教师的尊重。
This is to show respect for the teacher.

善学者，师逸而功倍，又从而庸之；不善学者，师勤而功半，又从而怨之。善问者如攻坚木，先其易者，后其节目，及其久也，相说以解.；不善问者反此。善答问者如撞钟，叩之以小者则小鸣，叩之以大者则大鸣，待其从容，然后尽其声.；不善答问者反此。此皆进学之道也。

善于学习的人，教师安闲，而教育效果反而加倍，学生都归功于教师教导有方；
A teacher whose students are quick learners will be at leisure. But their academic achievements will be twice as good. The students all attribute their good performance to the teacher.

不善于学习的人，教师督促严厉，而教育效果只有一半，学生都怨恨教师过于苛刻。
A teacher has to be strict with those of his students who are not good at studying. But their academic achievements will not be half as good. The students all hate the teacher for being too strict with them.

再抄十遍！
Copy this ten times.

善于发问的人，如锯坚硬的木头，先从较软处入手，而及较硬的节疤，时间久了，木头自然分开。不善于发问的人，则与此相反。

For a good student asking questions is like sawing hard wood. He starts from the relatively soft spot and work his way to the hard knot. If he saws long enough, the wood will come apart. For a person who is not good at asking questions it is just the opposite.

善于答问的人，有如撞钟，轻轻敲击，钟声也小，重重撞击，钟声则大。

A person good at answering questions is like ringing a bell. If you hit it light, the sound is small; you hit it hard, the sound is loud.

一定要从容不迫，钟声才会余韵悠扬。
Hit it calmly and the bell will emit a melodious sound.

不善答问的人则相反。这些都是增进学问的方法。

A person not good at answering questions is just the opposite. Here we talked about the method for improving your study.

为什么？
Why?

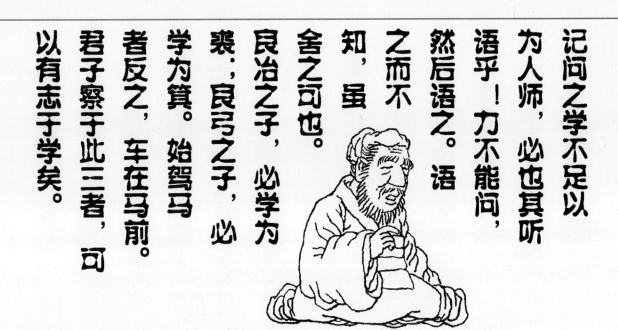

记问之学不足以为人师，必也其听语乎！力不能问，然后语之。语之而不知，虽舍之可也。良冶之子，必学为裘；良弓之子，必学为箕。始驾马者反之，车在马前。君子察于此三者，可以有志于学矣。

一味死记硬背，而没有独到见解的人，没有资格做别人的老师。
A person who learns by rote without his own ideas is not qualified to be a teacher.

一定要等到学生发问，再予以解答。
You must not give your answer until the student asks.

学生心存疑难，而没有能力表达，老师才加以开导；老师加以开导，学生仍不能明白，只有暂时放弃，以待将来。
If a student has questions but somehow doesn't know how to ask the questions, then the teacher will give him some guidance. If the student still doesn't understand, the teacher will just give up and leave the matter for a later date.

好铁匠的儿子，一定能补缀皮衣；
The son of a good blacksmith can certainly patch up a fur coat.

好弓匠的儿子，一定也能编织畚箕；
The son of a good bow maker can certainly weave a wicker scoop.

刚学驾车的小马，都先拴在车子后面，而车子在它前面。
A young horse which has just been taught how to pull a cart will be attached to the rear of the cart so the cart will be in front of the horse.

君子观察这三件事，就可以立定学习的志向了。
Having observed these three matters, a gentleman will set his goals for learning.

古之学者，比物丑类。鼓无当于五声，五声弗得不和；水无当于五色，五色弗得不章。；学无当于五官，五官弗得不治；师无当于五服，五服弗得不亲。

古代的学者，能够比较事物的异同，而触类旁通。如鼓的声音并不相当于五音中的任何一种，但是五者迭奏，没有鼓的调节就不能协调。

Through comparing things to find out their similarities and differences, ancient scholars comprehended by analogy. Take the drum for example. Its sound is not similar to any of the five notes of the pentatonic scale. But if you play a tune using the five notes without the adjustment of the drum, the tune would not sound coherent.

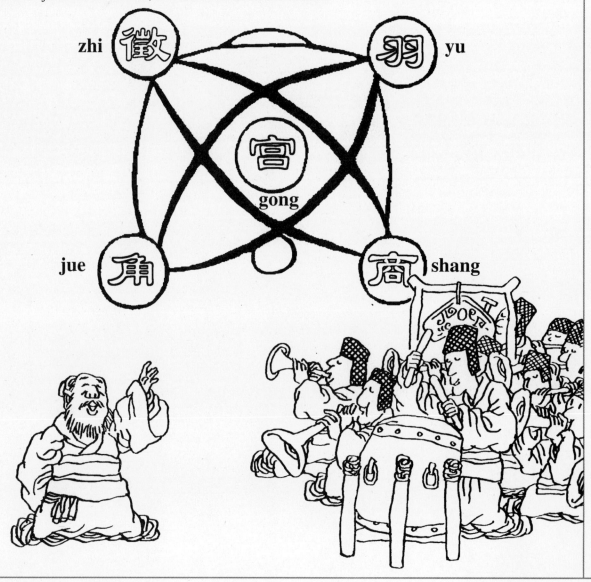

zhi 徵　羽 yu

宫 gong

jue 角　商 shang

又如水，水的颜色并不相当于五色当中的任何一色，然而五色的配合不通过水调剂就不能彰显。
Look at another example. The color of water is not similar to any of the five colors. But without water you can't mix any of the five colors to make a new color.

至于学者并不相当于政府的任何一种职务，然而任何一种职务不经过学习都不会办事。
A scholar is not tantamount to any of the official post in the government. But no government official can do his work well without first serving as a student.

再如老师，他不属于"五服"这一人伦关系中的任何一类亲属，但是任何亲属如果未经老师的教诲，也就不懂人伦关系了。
Teachers do not belong to any of the kith and kin. But without the education of teachers, no one in your kinship will understand human relations.

君子曰：大德不官，
大道不器，大信不约，
大时不齐。察
于此四者，
可以有志
于本矣。

有修养的人说：伟大的道德不偏治于某一种官职。
The wise man said, "Great morality is not exclusively associated with one official position."

普遍的道理，不局限于某一种事物。
General principles are not limited to one particular thing.

最大的诚信，不必载于盟书。
The greatest honesty need not necessarily be written in an agreement of alliance.

恒久的天时，不尽作用于某一个季节。
A certain type of weather may not always appear in a particular season.

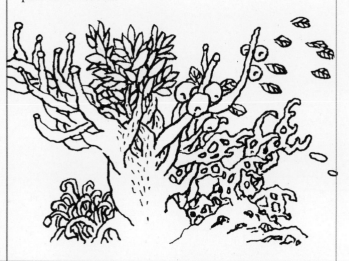

明白了这四种道理，就可以立志于学习了。
When you understand these four truths, you can make up your mind to concentrate on studying.

礼记图典

116

祭 义

祭义探讨的本是各种祭祀的意义。其中,以论述祭祀祖先的较多,但所含内容却甚为庞杂,超出了本来范围。如本章截取的曾子有关孝子事亲的议论,就是后世研究孝道及其实质的一篇重要文献资料,现在来看,仍然有着很强的现实意义。

The Meaning of Sacrificial Offering Rituals

The document entitled *jiyi* largely discusses the meaning of sacrificial offering rituals, with passages predominantly talking about offering sacrifices to ancestors. In fact the content is copious and chaotic, going beyond the original boundary. In this part we have taken some comments made by Zengzi about a filial son serving his parents. It is important material for the study of filial duty and its nature. The stories are relevant even today.

曾子曰：孝有三：
大孝尊亲，其次
弗辱，其下能养。
公明仪问于曾子曰：
夫子可以
为孝乎？
曾子曰：
是何言与？
是何言与！君子之
所谓孝者，先意承
志，谕父母于道。
参直养者也，
安能为孝乎？

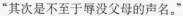

曾子说："孝有三等，大孝是能使父母得到天下人的尊敬。"
Zengzi said, "Filial piety can be rated in three grades. Great filial piety will win your parents the respect of everyone in the country."

"其次是不至于辱没父母的声名。"
"Not sullying the reputation of one's parents comes next."

没辙！
I am at my wits' end.

就是说，我不给父母惹事儿。
That means I shall not make any trouble for my parents.

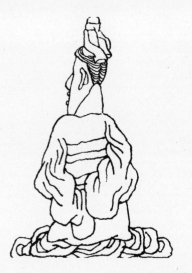

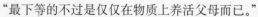

"最下等的不过是仅仅在物质上养活父母而已。"
"The lowest grade of filial piety is to provide your parents with enough to eat."

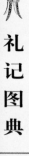

公明仪向曾子问道：
Gong Mingyi asked Zengzi,

像老师这样，算是孝子了吧？
Can a person like you be considered a filial son?

这是哪里的话？
No.

有修养的人所称为孝的，是在父母没有表示自己的意愿之前，做儿子的就预先按照父母的意愿去做了。
What a gentleman considers filial piety is like this: the son does what his parents wish him to do before they express such wishes.

而且又能使父母明白那是做人的正理。
What's more, he should also make them understand that he knows what hc docs is the right thing.

像我曾参这样，只能是在物质上养活父母而已，怎能称得上孝呢？
I can only support my parents physically. This alone cannot be called filial piety.

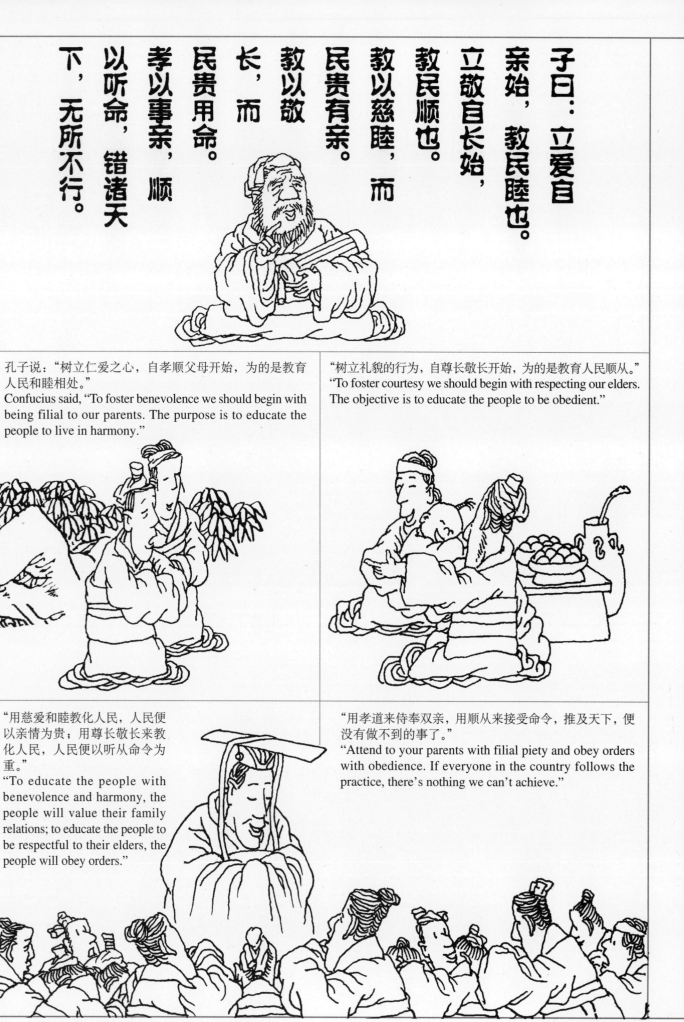

子曰：立爱自亲始，教民睦也。立敬自长始，教民顺也。教以慈睦，而民贵有亲。教以敬长，而民贵用命。孝以事亲，顺以听命，错诸天下，无所不行。

孔子说："树立仁爱之心，自孝顺父母开始，为的是教育人民和睦相处。"
Confucius said, "To foster benevolence we should begin with being filial to our parents. The purpose is to educate the people to live in harmony."

"树立礼貌的行为，自尊长敬长开始，为的是教育人民顺从。"
"To foster courtesy we should begin with respecting our elders. The objective is to educate the people to be obedient."

"用慈爱和睦教化人民，人民便以亲情为贵；用尊长敬长来教化人民，人民便以听从命令为重。"
"To educate the people with benevolence and harmony, the people will value their family relations; to educate the people to be respectful to their elders, the people will obey orders."

"用孝道来侍奉双亲，用顺从来接受命令，推及天下，便没有做不到的事了。"
"Attend to your parents with filial piety and obey orders with obedience. If everyone in the country follows the practice, there's nothing we can't achieve."

曾子曰：身也者，父母之遗体也。行父母之遗体，敢不敬乎？居处不庄，非孝也。事君不忠，非孝也。莅官不敬，非孝也。朋友不信，非孝也。战陈无勇，非孝也。五者不遂，灾及于亲，敢不敬乎？

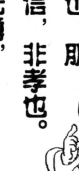

曾子说："人的身体，是父母所生，用父母所给的身体去做事，怎敢不敬呢？"
Zengzi said, "A person's body is given by his/her parents. We dare not do disrespectful things with the body bestowed by our parents."

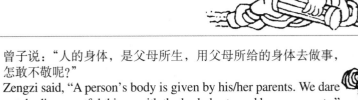

曾子

日常起居不庄重，就是不孝；
"Frivolous behaviors in daily life are not filial."

为国家做事不忠诚，就是不孝；
"Being disloyal to your country is not filial."

为官不恪尽职守，是不孝；
"An official who fails to perform his duty devotedly is not filial."

在战场上作战缺乏勇气，就是不孝。
"Showing no courage when you fight in the battlefield is not filial."

与朋友交往不讲信用，就是不孝；
"Never keeping your promises to your friends is not filial."

这五点都做不到，不仅自身要受到法律惩罚，还会给父母带来
灾祸，怎能不谨慎地对待呢？
If you fail to do these five points, you will not only be punished by
the law, but will also bring disaster upon your parents. So we should
be prudent when it comes to these five points."

亨孰羶芗，尝而荐之，非孝也，养也。君子之所谓孝也者，国人称愿然曰：幸哉有子如此。所谓孝也已。众之本教曰孝，其行曰养。养可能也，敬为难。敬可能也，安为难。安可能也，卒为难。

把饭菜做熟，尝过后端给父母，这还不能就算是孝，仅仅是赡养。
To prepare a meal, then try the dishes before taking them to your parents is not enough to be called filial piety. It is just providing for them.

君子所谓"孝"，是指国中的人都说：有这样的儿子多有福气啊！
Filial piety as considered by a gentleman is when everyone in the country says, "What good luck to have such a son."

能够如此，才算是孝子啊！
A person who wins such accolade can be called a real filial son.

对民众基本的教育是"孝"，表现在行为上是奉养双亲。
The basic teaching to the general public is that of filial piety. That means people are required to take good care of their parents.

奉养双亲，一般人都能做到，但尊敬父母，就不易做到。
Most people are willing to provide for their parents. But it's more difficult to profess respect for your parents.

充满敬意地奉养父母，即使做到了，而做得自然而然，应当应分，就比较难了。
Even if one can provide for one's parents with great respect, it would be more difficult if he does this naturally — rather than his duty.

能够自然而然，应当应分地敬养父母，并且一直始终如一，那就更难了。
It is even more difficult for a person to provide for his parents naturally, devotedly and consistently.

父母爱之，喜而
弗忘。父母
恶之，惧而
无怨。父母有过，
谏而不逆。
父母既
没，必
求仁者之粟
以祀之，此之
谓礼终。

父母给我慈爱，应当高兴，并且永远不忘；
You should be thankful for the love your parents give you and never forget it.

父母对我烦恶，应当戒惧并且毫不埋怨。
You should be aware of what they dislike about you but never complain about it.

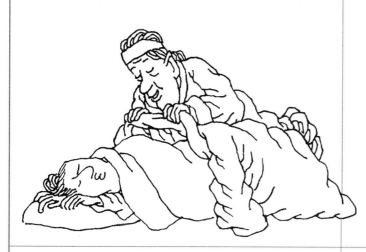

父母即便有过失，也应婉言相劝而不悖逆。
Even if your parents make a mistake, you should gently persuade them to correct the mistake, instead of defying them.

父母故去必须用自己正当的收入来祭祀他们，这才算是最终尽了孝道。
When your parents die, you should offer sacrifices to them using your legitimate income, completing your last filial duty.

乐正子春下堂而伤其足，数月不出，犹有忧色。门弟子曰：夫子之足瘳矣，数月不出，犹有忧色，何也？乐正子春曰：善如尔之问也！吾闻诸曾子，曾子闻诸夫子曰：天之所生，地之所养，无人为大。父母全而生之，子全而归之，可谓孝矣。不亏其体，不辱其身，可谓孝矣。故君子顷步而弗敢忘孝也。今予忘孝之道，予是以有忧色也。壹举足而不敢忘父母，壹出言而不敢忘父母。壹举足而不敢忘父母，是故道而不径，舟而不游，不敢以先父母之遗体行殆。壹出言而不敢忘父母，是故恶言不出于口，忿言不反于身。不辱其身，不羞其亲，可谓孝矣。

乐正子春有一次从堂上走下来时，不慎崴了脚，一连在家躺了几个月。伤好后仍然面带忧色，他门下的弟子很不解。
One day Yuezheng Zichun accidentally sprained his ankle when he stepped into the main room. He lay in bed for several months. He still appeared upset when he recovered from the injury. His disciples were puzzled.

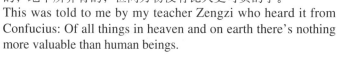

我从老师曾子那里听说，曾子是从孔子那里听说：天上所生长的，地下所养育的，世间万物没有比人更可贵的了。
This was told to me by my teacher Zengzi who heard it from Confucius: Of all things in heaven and on earth there's nothing more valuable than human beings.

父母把子女完完整整地生下来，子女百年时也应当完完整整地还给父母，这就是"孝"。
When parents give birth to a son or daughter, it comes to this world as a complete human being. When the son or daughter comes to the end of their life, they should give them back to their parents intact. This is filial piety.

一路平安！
Bon voyage!

多保重！
Take care!

不损害自己的身体，不辱没自己的名声，就算是做到了"全"。
Not harming your body or tarnishing your reputation — this is "quan."

所以有教养的人每走半步路，都不敢忘记孝道。
Well-educated people will never forget filial piety.

这次我忘记了孝道，因而感到很懊恼。
I feel upset because I forgot filial piety this time.

每走一步路都不敢忘记父母，每说一句话都不敢忘记父母。
I think of my parents when I take a step or when I say a word.

这就是说：一举足都不敢忘记父母，所以行路走大路不走小路。
That means every time I lift my feet I will not forget my parents. So I take the main road rather than the little path.

渡河要乘船，而不要凫水。
When crossing a river, I will ride in a ferry rather than swimming across.

不敢用父母给予的身体去做不必要的冒险行为。
I will not take unnecessary risks with the body bestowed to me by my parents.

一开口都不敢忘记父母，所以骂人的话不会出口。
I remember my parents whenever I open my mouth (to speak), so I will not utter curses.

于是别人也不会用脏话来骂自己。
As a result, other people will not curse me.

不辱没自身，不使父母蒙羞，这就算是孝子了。
Do not bring disgrace upon yourself or your parents, and you will be called a filial son.

经　解

　　经解是对儒家六经，即：《诗》、《书》、《礼》、《乐》、《易》、《春秋》的题解。阐述了六经在中国古代教育中的不同目的和效果。本篇前半部分是总论六经的宗旨与得失，后半部分是强调"礼"对于治理国家、人民的重大意义和作用，以及如何用礼义来教化民众。

Explanation of the Classics

The classics refer to the six books of the Confucian School: *The Book of Songs, The Book of History, The Book of Rites, The Book of Music, The Book of Changes* and *The Spring and Autumn Annals*. This part explains the aims and effects of the six classics in China's ancient education. The first half talks about the purposes of the six classics as well as their successes and failures. The second half emphasizes the great significance and function of rite in governing a country and managing its people. It also discusses how to educate the people with rites.

经解

孔子曰：入其国，其教可知也。其为人也，温柔敦厚，《诗》教也；疏通知远，《书》教也；广博易良，《乐》教也；洁静精微，《易》教也；恭俭庄敬，《礼》教也；属辞比事，《春秋》教也。

孔子说："到了一个国家，是可以看出那里的教化实施情况的。"
Confucius said, "You can tell the effects of education in a country when you are in that country."

"国家和人民的风俗气质，如果是温柔而敦厚的，那是用《诗》来进行教化的。"
"If people in a country are gentle and honest, then they must have received education using *The Book of Songs*."

"通达政事，而且了解历史的，那是用《书》来进行教化的。"
"If the people are well versed in political affairs and history, then they must have received education using *The Book of History*."

"清静致远，而又懂得哲理，那是用《易》来进行教化的。"
"If people are peaceful of mind and knowledgeable about philosophy, then they must have received education using *The Book of Changes*."

"如果是谦恭、俭朴而且庄重，那是用《礼》来进行教化的。"
"If people are modest, thrifty and dignified, then they must have received education using *The Book of Rites*."

"如果是广博而文雅，那是用《乐》来进行教化的。"
"If people are erudite and refined in manner, then they must have received education using *The Book of Music*."

"善于言辞，借鉴历史，那是用《春秋》来进行教化的。"
"If people are articulate and tend to draw lessons from history, then they must have received education using *The Spring and Autumn Annals*."

故《诗》之失愚；《书》之失诬；《乐》之失奢，《易》之失贼；《礼》之失烦；《春秋》之失乱。其为人也，温柔敦厚而不愚，则深于《诗》者也；疏通知远而不诬，则深于《书》者也；广博易良而不奢，则深于《乐》者也；洁静精微而不贼，则深于《易》者也；恭俭庄敬而不烦，则深于《礼》者也；属辞比事而不乱，则深于《春秋》者也。

所以《诗》教的缺陷，在于缺少理智；
The flaw of education by *The Book of Songs* is the lack of rationality.

《书》教的缺陷，在于言过其实；
The flaw of education by *The Book of History* is overstatement.

《乐》教的缺陷，在于过分奢侈；
The flaw of education by *The Book of Music* is extravagance.

《易》教的缺陷，在于导致迷信；
The flaw of education by *The Book of Changes* is that it leads to superstition.

《礼》教的缺陷，是流于烦琐；
The flaw of education by *The Book of Rites* is that it is loaded down with trivial details.

《春秋》教的缺陷，是以文乱法。
The flaw of education by *The Spring and Autumn Annals* is that it makes people confused.

爷爷说过，心诚才是最重要的。
Grandpa said the most important thing is to be honest.

导致混乱。
It leads to confusion.

一个国家的人民，既温柔敦厚，而又不愚笨迟钝，那是深得《诗》教的；
When the people of a country are gentle and honest, but not stupid or slow, then it's an indication they have been educated by *The Book of Songs*.

如果是通达知古而又不言过其实，那是深得于《书》道的；
If they are sensible, knowledgeable about the past and do not make overstatements, that's an indication they have been educated by *The Book of History*.

如果是宽宏博雅，平易善良而又不过分奢侈，那是深得于《乐》教的；

If they are open-minded, refined in manner, easy-going and kind-hearted, yet not excessively extravagant, then it's an indication they have been educated by *The Book of Music*.

如果是富于哲理而又未导致迷信，那是深得于《易》教的；

If they are versed in philosophical theories but do not believe in superstition, then it's an indication they have been educated by *The Book of Changes*.

易学是我们面对世界的一种立场、观点和方法。
The Book of Changes talks about our stand, viewpoint and method about the world.

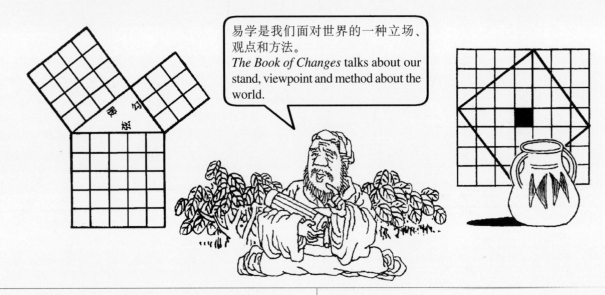

谦恭、俭朴、庄重而又不烦琐，那是深得于《礼》教的；

If people are modest, thrifty and dignified yet not fastidious about trivial details, then it's an indication they have been educated by *The Book of Rites*.

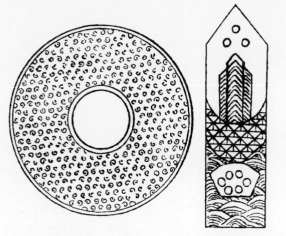

善于言辞和分析问题，而又不失条理，那是深得于《春秋》教化的。

If people are articulate, good at analyzing problems in a rational manner, then it's an indication they have been educated by *The Spring and Autumn Annals*.

天子者，与天地参，故德配天地，兼利万物，与日月并明，明照四海而不遗微小。

其在朝廷，则道仁圣礼义之序；燕处，则听《雅》、《颂》之音；行步，则有环佩之声；升车，则有鸾和之音。居处有礼，进退有度，百官得其宜，万事得其序。

天子，就是与天地相参验的意思。

An emperor is also referred to as the "Son of Heaven" because he is supposed to have learnt from the rules governing the functions of heaven and earth.

所以，天子的德行应与天地相一致。

So what the emperor does should be in accordance with the rules of heaven and earth.

恩泽遍及万物，同太阳和月亮一样明亮，普照四海，无微不至。

He bestowed bounties on all living things, shining brightly like the sun and moon on the four oceans, without missing the minuscule places.

他在朝廷之上，则以仁爱、圣明、礼义示范臣下；
In court he is benevolent, wise and courteous — setting a good example to his ministers.

在休息时，则欣赏文雅祥和的音乐；外出行走，身上的佩饰铿铿作响；
When he is taking a rest he listens to beautiful and auspicious music; when he takes a stroll outside, the jewelry he wears gives out a nice sound.

登车时，车铃发出有节奏的和谐之声。
When he rides in a carriage, the bells on the carriage give out a nice rhythmic note.

起居有仪，进退从容，百官尽职，万事有条理。
He leads his daily life in grand style and does everything in a leisurely way. All his ministers and officials perform their duties diligently. All business of the country is done in the right order.

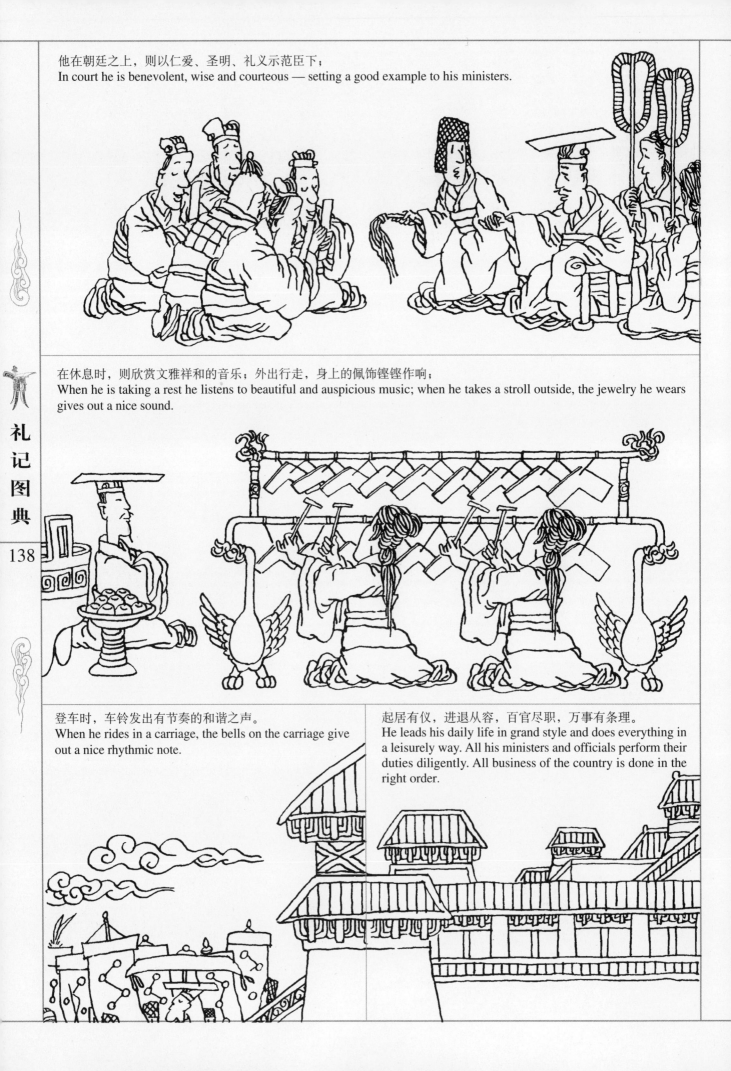

《诗》云：「淑人君子，其仪不忒，其仪不忒，正是四国」。此之谓也。发号出令而民说，谓之和；上下相亲，谓之仁；民不求其所欲而得之，谓之信；除去天地之害，谓之义。义与信，和与仁，霸王之器也。有治民之意而无其器，则不成。

《诗经》中说："君主文雅，仪表有度，四方各国就会得到治理。"说的就是这个道理。
The Book of Songs says, "When a monarch is suave and carries himself in an elegant way, the states on all four sides are managed well." This refers to the situation we have just talked about.

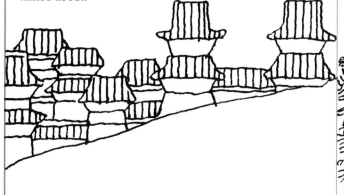

天子发布号令而人民喜悦，这就叫做"和"。
The emperor issues an order and the people are happy about it — this is called he, or harmony.

上下相亲相爱，这叫做"仁"。
The superiors and subordinates love each other — this is called ren, or benevolence.

我代表政府……
On behalf of the government, I....

人民不待要求便已得到好处，这叫做"信"。
People's demands are met before they make their requests — this is called xin, or trust.

避除自然灾害，这叫做"义"。
Preventing the country from suffering natural disasters is called yi or righteousness.

义与信，是霸主的器具。
Yi and xin are the tools of a ruler.

有治理人民的愿望而没有所需的器具，则不能达到目的。
Although you may desire to govern the people, you won't attain your goal if you don't have the necessary tools.

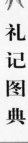

和与仁，是王者的器具。
He and ren are the tools of a monarch.

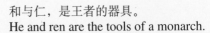

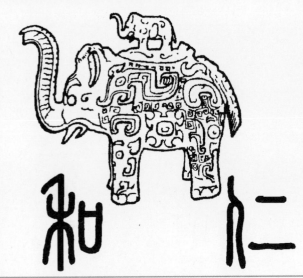

礼之于正国也，犹衡
之于轻重也，绳墨
之于曲直也，
规矩之于方圆也。
故衡诚县，不可欺
以轻重；绳墨诚陈，
不可欺以曲直；
规矩诚设，不可
欺以方圆；
君子审礼，
不可诬以奸诈。是
故隆礼由礼，谓之
有方之士；不隆礼、不
由礼，谓之无方之民。

"礼"对于治理国家，犹如用称来称量轻重，用绳墨来矫正曲直，用规矩来画方圆。
The rites used in governing a country are just like weighing things with scales, making straight lines with a carpenter's ruler or drawing circles with a compass and squares with a ruler.

所以，天秤准确地悬在那里，就难以用轻重来欺人；
If a pair of scales was available, it would be hard for anyone who wanted to lie about the weight.

绳墨准确地摆放在那里，就难以用曲直来欺人。
If carpenter's ruler was on hand, it would be hard for anyone to insist that a crooked line was straight.

准确使用圆规和矩尺，就难以用方圆来欺人。
The correct use of a pair of compasses and rulers would make it hard for anyone who wished to cheat people about a circle or square.

君子用礼仪来审察一切，小人就难以用虚妄来施行奸诈。
When a gentleman examines everything with rites, then a wicked person would find it difficult to carry out his deception with false pretenses.

因而，重视"礼"，并按照"礼"的标准行事，就是正直的人；
So a person who attaches importance to rites and does things according to the principles of rites is an honest person.

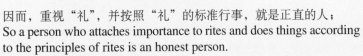

轻视"礼"，并且不按照"礼"的标准做事，那就不是正直的人。
A person who despises rites and does not do things according to the principles of rites is not an honest person.

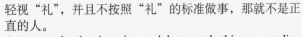

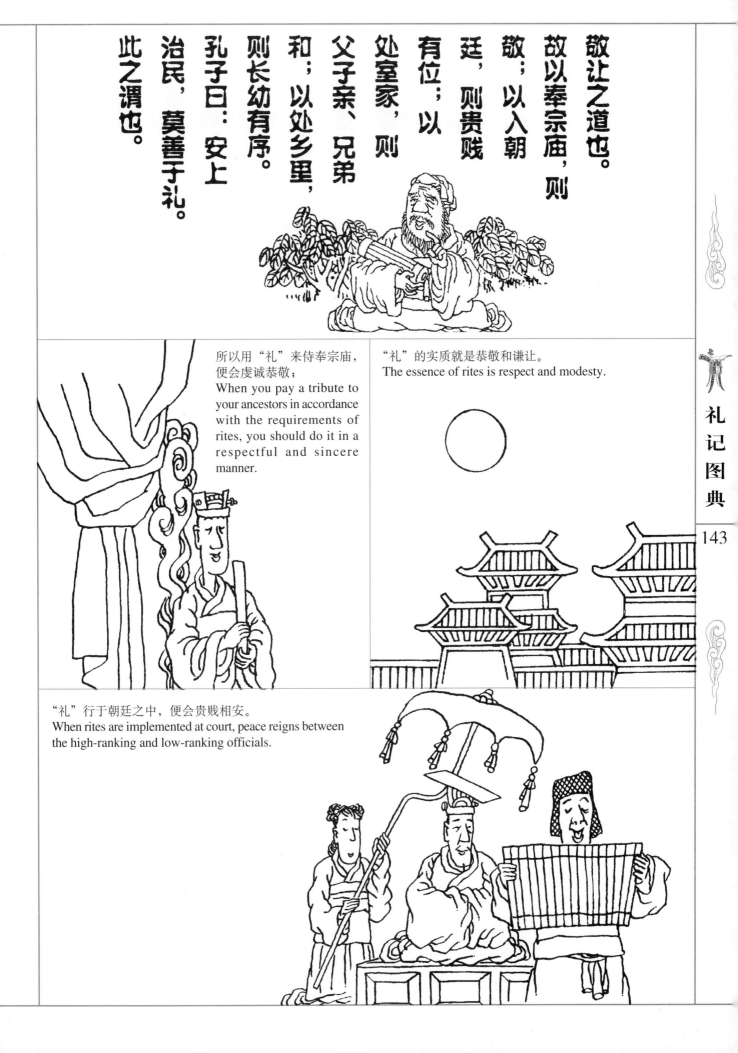

敬让之道也。故以奉宗庙，则敬；以入朝廷，则贵贱有位；以处室家，则父子亲、兄弟和；以处乡里，则长幼有序。孔子曰：安上治民，莫善于礼。此之谓也。

"礼"的实质就是恭敬和谦让。
The essence of rites is respect and modesty.

所以用"礼"来侍奉宗庙，便会虔诚恭敬；
When you pay a tribute to your ancestors in accordance with the requirements of rites, you should do it in a respectful and sincere manner.

"礼"行于朝廷之中，便会贵贱相安。
When rites are implemented at court, peace reigns between the high-ranking and low-ranking officials.

"礼"行于家庭内，便会使父子亲爱，兄弟和睦；
When rites are implemented within a family, father and son will love each other and there will be harmony between brothers.

孔子说："安定君长，治理人民，没有比礼更好的方法了。"
讲的正是这个意思。
Just as Confucius said, "Nothing is better than rites to put the chief at ease and to govern the people."

"礼"行于乡党邻里之间，便会长幼有序，井然不乱。
When rites are implemented in a community or village, the relations between the old and young will be in good order.

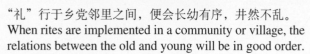

故朝觐之礼，所以明君臣之义也；聘问之礼，所以使诸侯相尊敬也；丧祭之礼，所以明臣子之恩也；乡饮酒之礼，所以明长幼之序也；昏姻之礼，所以明男女之别也。夫礼禁乱之所由生，犹坊止水之所自来也。

因此，诸侯朝见天子的礼仪，是用来显示君臣身份不同。
The rites with respect to a minister's audience with the emperor are used to show the different status of a monarch and his ministers.

诸侯之间相互聘问的礼仪，是为了使诸侯相互尊敬。
The rites governing dukes and princes when they pay respects to each other are used to show their mutual respect.

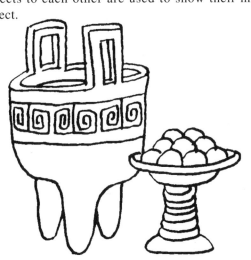

丧礼与祭礼，是为了表明为臣、为子的人不忘恩情。
Rites such as funerals and sacrificial offerings show the ministers' or sons' gratitude to a dead sovereign or parent.

礼记图典

145

婚姻的仪礼，是用以显示男女之间的区别。
The rites of a wedding are used to show the difference between men and women.

礼是用来禁绝祸乱发生的根源。
Rites are used to prevent catastrophes from occurring.

乡饮酒的仪礼，是用以显示长辈与晚辈间的伦序。
The rites governing a drinking party in the village are used to demonstrate the appropriate relations between the old and young.

就像用堤防来防止洪水泛滥一样。
Just like dams are used to prevent floods.

故以旧坊为无所用而坏之者，必有水败；以旧礼为无用而去之者，必有乱患。故昏姻之礼废，则夫妇之道苦，而淫辟之罪多矣；乡饮酒之礼废，则长幼之序失，而争斗之狱繁矣；丧祭之礼废，则臣子之恩薄，而倍死忘生者众矣；聘、觐之礼废，则君臣之位失，诸侯之行恶，而倍畔侵凌之败起矣。

以为旧有的堤坝无用而毁坏它，必然要遭受洪水的灾害；
If you destroy the old dams because you think they are useless you will certainly cause catastrophic flooding.

以为旧有的礼法无用而废弃它，也必然会有祸乱发生。
If you abrogate the old rites because you think they are unnecessary disasters will certainly occur.

所以，废弃婚姻之礼，则夫妻之间便很难相处，而易发生淫奔苟合之罪。
So when marriage rites are ignored, it would be hard for the husband and wife to get along and it is very likely that adultery would ensue.

惭愧了！
What a shame.

废弃乡饮酒的礼仪，便会失去长者与晚辈之间的秩序，
Abolish the rites governing the village drinking party and the good order between the old and young will disappear.

从而发生许多争斗和狱讼官司。
Fighting and lawsuits will ensue.

废弃丧祭之礼，做臣子的便会寡恩薄义，变成背叛死者、忘记祖先的人。
Abolish the rites for funerals and sacrificial offerings and ministers and sons will become ungrateful people. They will betray the dead and forget their ancestors.

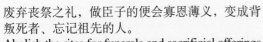

废弃朝觐、聘问的礼仪，便会失去君臣、上下的身份。诸侯们便会出现背信弃义，相互侵害的事情了。
Abolish the rites concerning a minister's audience with his monarch or dukes paying respects to each other and the proper social status of monarchs and ministers and dukes will no longer exist. Then some dukes and princes may break their faith and try to overthrow their rivals.

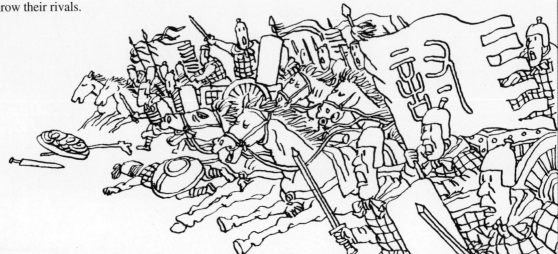

仲尼燕居

　　仲尼燕居记述的是孔子日常与弟子们的问答之辞，主要内容是"礼"与从政的关系。提出了"即事之治也"的论断，指出"治国而无礼，譬犹瞽之无相与？"孔子认为，"礼"是人们生活的依据。他说："礼也者，理也。"因此，"君子无理不动，无节不作"。

The Leisurely Life of Confucius

This part records the questions and answers between Confucius' disciples and Confucius in their daily life. It deals mainly with the relationship between rites and politics. Confucius advances the thesis that "rite means appropriateness." He compares the "governing of a country without rites to a blind person walking without help." Confucius believes that rites are the basis of people's life. He said, "Rites are rationale." So "a gentleman will not do things that are unreasonable; he will not act without the guidance of rites."

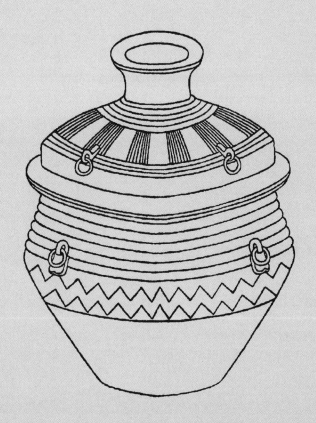

仲尼燕居

仲尼燕居，子张、子贡、言游侍，纵言至于礼。子曰：居，汝三人者！吾语女礼，使女以礼周流无不遍也。子贡越席而对曰：敢问何如？子曰：敬而不中礼谓之野，恭而不中礼谓之给，勇而不中礼谓之逆。子曰：给夺慈仁。

孔子有一天在家休息，他的弟子子张、子贡、子游在左右陪侍，谈话中说到了"礼"。
One day Confucius was taking a rest at home. His disciples Zizhang, Zigong and Ziyou are with him. Their conversation shifts to the subject of "rites."

礼记图典

150

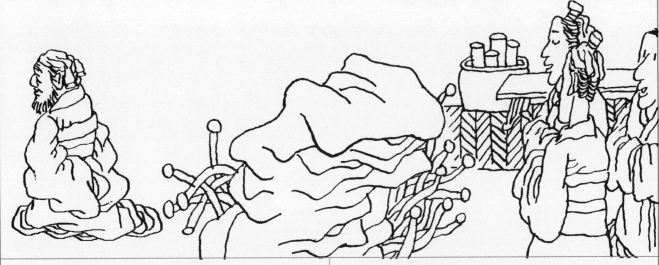

孔子说："你们三个人坐下，我告诉你们礼是怎么回事，使你们以礼处理一切。"
"You sit down," said Confucius. "I'll tell you what rites are about so that you'll deal with everything in accordance with the requirements of rites."

子贡首先离席问道："请问老师礼是怎样的呢？"
Zigong stands up and asks, "What are rites, sir?"

孔子说："敬而不合乎礼的规范，叫作粗野。"
Confucius said, "When someone wants to be respectful but his actions are not up to the standard of rites, it is called rudeness."

"勇武而不合乎礼的规范叫做粗暴。"
"When someone is valiant but his actions are not up to the standard of rites, it is called brutality."

"恭维而不合乎礼的规范，叫做巴结。"
"When someone wants to show his deference but his actions are not up to the standard of rites, it is called fawning."

孔子接着说："巴结往往会取代仁的本意。"
Then Confucius continued, "Fawning will normally replace the original meaning of benevolence."

没见过仁者会巧言令色，曲意逢迎的。
No benevolent person will use clever talk and ingratiate himself with other people against his own will.

"给"者，足恭便佞意，即巴结之貌。
Gei in classical Chinese means fawning.

在"野、给、逆"三者之间，孔子独言"给"之为害，是由于"野、逆"二者乃秉性使然，尚可通过"礼"来进行规范。
Of the three — rudeness, fawning, brutality — Confucius emphasizes the malicious effect of fawning because he believes that rudeness and brutality are natural dispositions which can be corrected by rites.

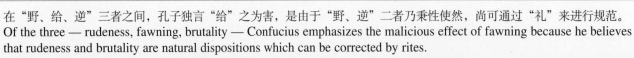

而巴结逢迎之徒，则曲意徇物，致饰于外，务以悦人；貌虽类于慈仁，内心实存私欲，故谓之"夺仁"。
But a flatterer will try to ingratiate himself with his superior. He may seem to be a kind person on the surface, but he has a hidden desire for personal gain. Therefore people will often mistake fawning for a genuine benevolent act.

子曰：礼者何也？即事之治也。君子有其事，必有其治。治国而无礼，譬犹瞽之无相与！伥伥乎其何之？譬如终夜有求于幽室之中，非烛何见？若无礼，则手足无所措，耳目无所加，进退揖让无所制。

孔子说："礼是什么?礼就是恰到好处，是得体。"
Confucius said, "What are rites? Rites are appropriateness. It's doing the right thing."

君子既然有自己的职守，就要有做好事情的方法。
Since a gentleman has his duties, he needs the means to perform his duties well.

治理国家没有"礼"，就好比盲者没有了扶持，迷迷惘惘不知向何处去。
Governing a country without rites is like a blind person walking without help. He will feel confused and won't know where to go.

我来也!
I am coming.

又好比整夜在暗室里寻找东西，没有烛光怎么会看得见呢？
Governing a country without rites is also like looking for something in a dark room. How can you see anything without candle light?

假若没有礼，就会不知如何举手投足。
Without rites people will not know how to comport themselves.

耳目也不知如何视听。
Without rites they will not know what to listen to and what to see.

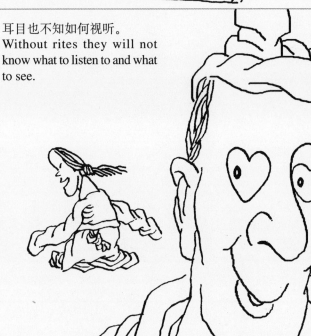

进退揖让也不知如何是好。
They will be at a loss to know how to interact with other people.

子曰：礼也者，理也。乐也者，节也。君子无礼不动，无节不作。不能《诗》，于礼缪。不能乐，于礼素。薄于德，于礼虚。

孔子说："所谓礼，就是理的意思。"
Confucius said, "Rites are rationale."

礼得其理，则有序而不乱。
With the rationale behind rites, order will be established to replace chaos.

"所谓乐，就是'节'的意思。"
"Yue (music) also means restraint."

乐得其节，则虽和而不流。
Restrained music is harmonious, and not vulgar.

"君子行为不合于礼不动，防的是乱。"
"A gentleman will not do things that are unappropriate to avoid chaos."

"情不合于节不做，防的是流。"
"He will not show excessive affection to avoid being flighty."

不懂《诗》，于礼就会悖谬。
If a person does not understand *The Book of Songs*, he will deviate from the right course when performing the rites.

不懂《乐》，于礼就会乏味。
If a person does not understand *The Book of Music*, he will feel bored when performing the rites.

德行不厚，于礼就会茫然。
A person without great virtues will feel puzzled when it comes to performing the rites.

子张问政。子曰：师乎，前吾语女乎！君子明于礼乐，举而错之而已。子张复问。子曰：师，尔以为必铺几筵，升降、酌献、酬酢，然后谓之礼乎？尔以为必行缀兆，兴羽龠，作钟鼓，然后谓之乐乎？言而履之，礼也。行而乐之，乐也。

子张问如何从事政事。孔子答道："到前面来，我告诉过你的。君子懂得礼乐的作用，不过是把它们运用到政事上。"
Then Zizhang asked Confucius about politics. Confucius said ,"A gentleman knows the function of rites and music. He will apply them to the administration of a country."

子张又问。孔子接着说："子张，你以为一定要摆设几案，升堂下阶，斟酒奉物，劝杯回盏，然后才叫礼吗？"
Zizhang asked some more questions. Confucius said, "Zizhang, do you think you must always set the table, go down the stairs to your seat in the main hall, pour wine and present food, toast your guests and then call all this rites?"

这才叫礼吗？
Do you call these rites?

"你以为一定要排列舞队、挥动羽龠、鸣钟击鼓，然后才叫做乐吗？"
"Do you think you must always have the dancing girls lined up in formation, waving their plumes while the musicians strike the chimes and beat the drums, and will you call that music?"

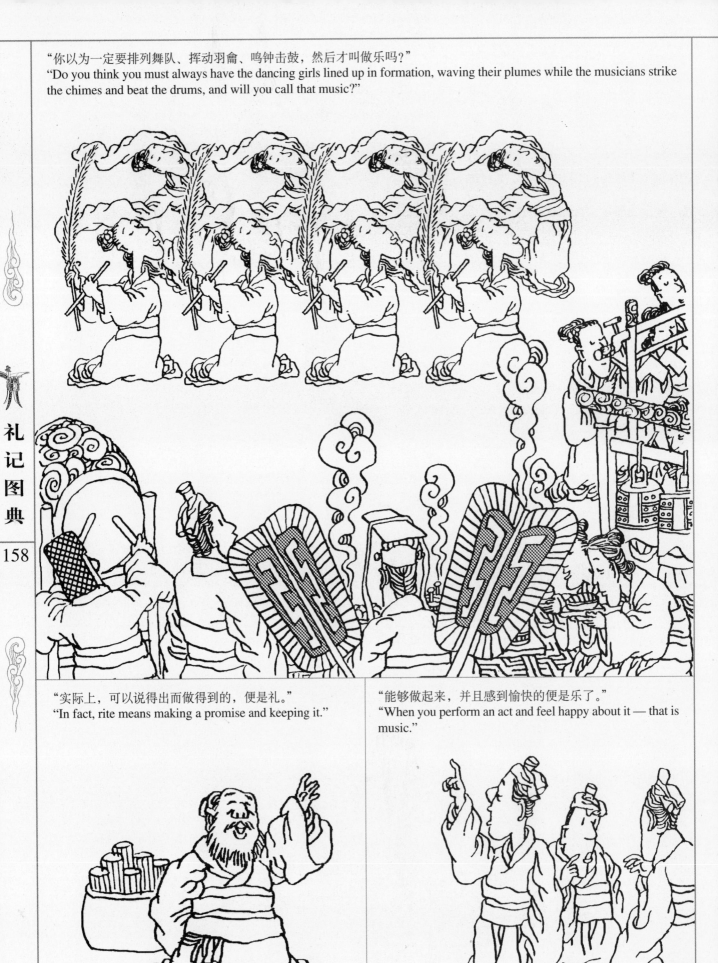

"实际上，可以说得出而做得到的，便是礼。"
"In fact, rite means making a promise and keeping it."

"能够做起来，并且感到愉快的便是乐了。"
"When you perform an act and feel happy about it — that is music."

儒　行

儒行篇由于历述儒者的行为，因而命名为儒行。篇中以鲁哀公问儒行于孔子，孔子历述儒者行为而成文。计有儒者的自立、容貌、备预、近人、特立、刚毅、仕、忧思、宽裕、任举、独行、规为、交友、尊让等十五项处世原则，表现了儒者既积极进取、又独立不阿的风范与气度。

The Behavior of a Confucian Scholar

This part talks about the behavior of a Confucian scholar. In the text Confucius gave detailed answers to the questions raised by Duke Ai of the State of Lu about the behavior of a Confucian scholar. His answer covers 15 principles adopted by a Confucian scholar in conducting himself and dealing with the outside world, including his political aspirations and theories, some pronounced features of his character, and so on. It displays the enterprising spirit of a Confucian scholar, and also his belief about remaining independent and maintaining his integrity.

鲁哀公问于孔子曰：夫子之服，其儒服与？孔子对曰：丘少居鲁，衣逢掖之衣。长居宋，冠章甫之冠。丘闻之也：君子之学也博，其服也乡。丘不知儒服。

鲁哀公对孔子问道："先生所穿的衣服，是儒者所特有的吗？"
Duke Ai of the State of Lu asked Confucius, "Are the clothes you are wearing exclusive to Confucian scholars?"

孔子答道："我少年居住在鲁国，穿的是腋下肥大的衣服。长大后居住在宋国，戴着殷代样式的章甫帽。"
Confucius answered, "I lived in the State of Lu when I was a child. At that time I wore baggy clothes. Then I moved to the State of Song and wore a hat like the Zhangfu hat worn by people in the Yin Dynasty."

我听说，君子的学问要渊博，衣服要入乡随俗，
It is said that a gentleman must be taught; his clothes will be the same as those in his community.

我不知道什么是儒者所特有的服装。
I haven't heard anything about special clothes for Confucian scholars.

哀公曰：敢问儒
行。孔子对曰：
遽数之，不
能终其物。悉数之，
乃留，更仆未
可终也。哀公
命席，孔
子侍曰：
儒有席上
之珍以待聘，
夙夜强学以待问，
怀忠信以待举，
力行以待取。
其自立有如此者。

哀公问道："请您谈谈儒者的行为。"
Duke Ai asked, "Please say something about the role of a Confucian scholar."

这个问题很笼统，仓促之间不能
一一尽述，那样会花很多时间，到
仆人换班也讲不完。
This is a rather general question. If I go into detail, it will take a long time. I won't finish until the servants change shifts.

于是鲁哀公命人摆设坐席，孔子陪侍哀公，说：儒者有如这席上的珍品，可备他人聘用。
Then Duke Ai ordered his men to set the table and place some food on the table. Sitting down to keep Duke Ai company, Confucius said, "Confucian scholars are like the precious utensils on the table — ready to be employed by others."

早晚用功充实自己，以备他人的咨问。
"They study diligently day and night to increase their knowledge in case someone may come to consult them."

心怀忠信，以备他人的举荐。
"They remain loyal and trustworthy — ready for others to recommend them to the government."

努力修行，等待他人的录取。
"They cultivate their moral character waiting to be employed by others."

儒者的自修立身就是这样。
This is how Confucian scholars cultivate themselves.

儒者希望为人所用，但态度是有所待而无所求。
They want others to spot their talents and employ them, but they would wait for others to come to them rather than entreat others to do so.

礼记图典

162

儒有衣冠中，动作慎。其大让如慢，小让如伪，大则如威，小则如愧。其难进而易退也，粥粥若无能也。其容貌有如此者。

儒者穿戴的衣帽得中适度，行为谨慎，对大事的辞让，有如慢而不敬。对小事的辞让，虚辞即受，好像虚伪。对大事考虑再三，好像心存畏惧，对小事也不放任，好像心有愧疚。不与人争先，而讲究退让，有如柔弱无能的样子。

Confucian scholars wear proper clothes and hats, and act cautiously. When asked to take up matters of great significance, their initial refusal seems disrespectful. When asked to handle matters of little importance, they would decline first and then accept, as if they are hypocrites. They would deliberate on matters of great significance as if they are fearful of the matters. They handle matters of little importance conscientiously as if they have a sense of shame and remorse. They don't vie with other people to get ahead; instead they are willing to make a concession. They seem to be frail and incompetent.

三揖而后进，故说难进，一辞而遂退，故说易退。
It is difficult for them to get ahead because they will bow three times before advancing. It is easy for them to retreat because they will just decline and retreat.

儒者的容貌有这般的。
A Confucian scholar looks like this.

儒有居处齐难，其坐起恭敬，言必先信，行必中正，道涂不争险易之利，冬夏不争阴阳之和。爱其死以有待也，养其身以有为也。其备豫有如此者。

儒者日常起居，严肃端庄似有所畏难，坐立如仪。
Confucian scholars are serious and dignified in daily life. They act as if they are facing difficulties. They sit straight and walk in a dignified manner.

讲话必以信用为先，行为必以中正为要，路途中不争易避险而只图利己。
Their speech is credible; their behaviors are in line with standards of propriety. On a trip they would not vie with others for the dangerous or easy road if it is to their advantage.

冬夏不与人争处冷暖调和的地方，爱惜生命是为了等待机会的出现，调养身体是为了有所作为。
They will not vie with others for a comfortable place in winter or summer. They take good care of their life just to wait for an opportunity to come their way. They build up their health in order to do meritorious service.

儒者日常的修养有这样的。
This is the daily self-cultivation of Confucian scholars.

礼记图典

164

儒有不宝金玉，而忠
信以为宝；不祈
土地，立义以为土地；
不祈多积，多
文以为富。难得而
易禄也，易
禄而难畜
也。非时
不见，不亦
难得乎？非义
不合，不亦难畜乎？
先劳而后禄，
不亦易禄乎？其
近人有如此者。

儒者不以金玉为宝，而是以忠信为宝。
Confucian scholars value loyalty and trust more than gold or jade.

忠 信

不求有土地，而以义为土地。
They don't covet land; they consider righteousness their land.

義

不求积蓄财富，而以博学为富有。
They don't covet wealth; they consider knowledge their wealth.

儒者不计较个人得失，但非道不仕，所以难以得到而容易禄养。
They don't care about personal gains and losses. They will not hold an official post if they don't think they are serving the just cause. They are hard to come by but easy to employ.

容易禄养，但难于笼络，
They are easy to employ but difficult to win over.

我不能丢掉自己的独立人格。
I mustn't give up my own personality.

不到适当的时候不现身，这不是很难得到吗?
They will not come out until the critical moment. Therefore they are hard to come by.

不合于理，则不与君长合作，这不是很难笼络吗?
They will not work with a ruler if they think he is not pursuing the right cause. Therefore they are difficult to win over.

恕难从命！
I am sorry I can't accept the offer.

那小子竟敢鼓吹"民为贵，社稷次之，君为轻"！
How dare he say "people are the most valuable, followed by the state. The monarch comes last."

先做出成绩然后才领取酬劳，这不是很容易禄养?
They will render some meritorious service before collecting their payment. Therefore they are easy to employ.

儒者立身处世就是这样。
This is the way they conduct themselves in society.

儒有委之以货财，淹之以乐好，见利不亏其义。劫之以众，沮之以兵，见死不更其守。鸷虫攫搏不程勇者，引重鼎不程其力，往者不悔，来者不豫。过言不再，流言不极。不断其威，不习其谋。其特立有如此者。

儒者接受财物，会表现出高兴的样子，但不会见利而忘义。
Confucian scholars will be happy when they accept gifts. But they will not sacrifice principle for profit.

用众人威吓，以武力恐吓，也不会由于怕死而改变操守。
Intimidate them with a crowd or threaten them with force, and they will not alter their moral integrity for fear of death.

请您笑纳。
Here's a present for you.

遇到猛兽便上前搏斗，而不考虑自己的勇武能否胜任。
When they encounter a ferocious beast, they will fight it, without considering whether or not they are a match for it.

扛举重鼎也不考虑自己的力量是否够用；
When they lift a heavy ding (an ancient cooking vessel made of metal) they will not consider whether or not they are strong enough.

对过去的事情从不追悔，对未来的事情从不臆测；
They never regret things that happened in the past. Nor will they speculate about what will happen in the future.

而只管按固有信念去做。
I will do whatever I believe in.

讲过的话不再犹豫，对于谣言也不究其来源。
They will not dwell on what they have said. Nor will they try to find out the source of a rumor.

若无此事，谣言自灭，若有此事，又何必怕人评说？
If this never happened, the rumor would eventually subside. If this really happened, why should I be afraid of others' comments?

不以势压人、专断用事，也不热衷用伎俩侥幸成功。
They never use power to intimidate people. They will not act arbitrarily. Nor will they use crafty schemes in order to be successful.

儒者有这样特立独行的人。
Confucian scholars are as such independent people with their own principles.

儒有可亲而不可
劫也，可近而
不可迫也，
可杀而不可
辱也。其
居处不淫，
其饮食不溽。
其过失可微辨而不
可面数也。其刚
毅有如此者。

儒者可以亲密而不可以威胁。
You can be their best friend but you can't threaten them.

可以亲近而不可以强迫，可杀而不可侮辱。
You can have a close relationship with them but you can't force them to do what they are not willing to do. They would rather die than be humiliated.

礼记图典

169

他们居屋不求奢侈，饮食不求丰盛。他们的过失可以委婉地提示，而不可当面一一指责。儒者的刚毅有这样的。
They don't covet luxurious homes; they don't desire lavish meals. You can hint at their faults but not point them out in their face. In this way they are resolute people.

就是说，得给他点儿面子。
That is to say, we should let him keep face.

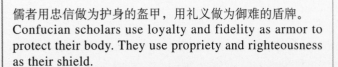

儒有忠信以为甲胄，礼义以为干橹。戴仁而行，抱义而处。虽有暴政，不更其所。其自立有如此者。儒有一亩之宫，环堵之室，筚门圭窬，蓬户瓮牖。易衣而出，并日而食。上答之不敢以疑，上不答不敢以谄。其仕有如此者。

儒者用忠信做为护身的盔甲，用礼义做为御难的盾牌。
Confucian scholars use loyalty and fidelity as armor to protect their body. They use propriety and righteousness as their shield.

行动或安居都以仁义为准则。
They follow the principle of benevolence and righteousness when they take actions or when they stay at home.

即使遇到暴政打击，也不更改原有的信念。
They will not renounce their original belief even if they suffer the blow of tyranny.

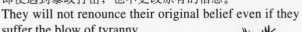

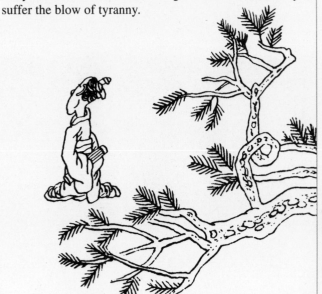

儒者的为人有这样的。
Confucian scholars are like this.

儒者中有这样的人，住宅占地一亩(东西南北各十步)，房间的周围是一堵(方丈为堵)宽，
There are some Confucian scholars whose house occupies a tract of land 1/15th of a hectare.

家人只有一套体面的衣服，出门换着穿用。
The family has only one smart set of clothes. Any member who goes out will wear this set of clothes.

两天只吃一日的食物。
For two days they eat food that is normally only enough for one day.

狭窄如圭的门户以荆竹和蓬草编成，不大的圆窗有如破瓮。
The gate is made of twigs, bamboo and grass woven together. The window is small and round.

上司提携时不敢迟疑，受冷落时也不谄媚巴结。
They dare not hesitate when their superiors give them a promotion. They will not make up to their superiors when they are slighted.

儒者对仕途(做官)的态度有这样的。
This is their attitude to bureaucratic jobs.

儒有今人与居，古人与稽。今世行之，后世以为楷。适弗逢世，上弗援，下弗推，谗谄之民有比党而危之者，身可危也，而志不可夺也。虽危起居，竟信其志，犹将不忘百姓之病也。其忧思有如此者。

儒者中有这样的人：与同时代的人相处，而稽考古人的行为。
Some Confucian scholars like to verify historical records about the actions of ancient people.

若是生不逢时，在上者不提携，在下者不举荐，
If they are not born in a good time, high-ranking officials will not help them get a promotion; low-ranking officials will not recommend them to the government.

并在当今的时代履行，被后世视为楷模。
Performing such an act in their time would be regarded as a good example by later generations.

虽可危害他们的身体，但不能动摇他们的意志。
The villains may harm their body, but they can't break their will.

又有搬弄是非的小人结党进行陷害。
Then some vile characters who like to speak ill of others form a clique to set the Confucian scholars up.

虽然日常生活遇到如此困厄，却依然坚持自己的信念。
Although they face such difficulties, they still stick to their convictions.

同时不忘记百姓的忧患。
Meanwhile, they are not forgetting the sufferings of ordinary people.

儒者的忧患意识有这样的。
Such are the Confucian scholars who are always concerned about the well-being of ordinary people.

儒有博学而不穷，笃行而不倦，幽居而不淫，上通而不困。礼之以和为贵，忠信之美，优游之法。慕贤而容众，毁方而瓦合。宽裕有如此者。其

礼记图典

儒者中有这样的人：学识广博而无穷尽，一心向善而不知疲倦。

They are erudite scholars who pursue good tirelessly.

独处时不放纵自己，通达于上时不背离道义。

They are not given to unbridled behavior when they are alone; they do not deviate from the just cause when they hold important government posts.

"礼"履行的精神以和谐为贵，以忠信为美，以宽厚为法度。

They observe the principles of rites. They value harmony, consider fidelity beautiful and maintain a standard of generosity and kindness.

羡慕贤者而容纳众人，既有原则又有灵活性。儒者的胸襟有这样的。

They admire virtuous and capable people and are tolerant of others. They have their principles as well as their flexibility. Confucian scholars are broad-minded in this way.

儒有内称不辟亲，
外举不辟怨。
程功积事，
推贤而
进达之，
不望其报。
君得其志。
苟利国家，不
求富贵。其举贤
援能有如此者。

儒者中有这样的人：向上举荐人才，内举不避嫌于亲属，外举不避嫌于怨仇，而是根据他们的功劳和行为，推荐贤者而使其得到任用，并不是希望得到报答。

Confucian scholars shun neither their relatives nor their rivals when making recommendations for official posts. Their recommendations are completely based on the performance of the candidate. They want virtuous and capable people to have an opportunity to serve the country. Reward is not what they want.

只是为了合乎君主的意志，确实有利于国家，而不是贪求个人的富贵。

They want to meet the wishes of the monarch, hoping their recommendation is in the interest of the country. They do not crave wealth and status.

儒者举贤荐能有这样的。

Confucian scholars will therefore recommend virtuous and capable people to the government.

儒有闻善以相告
也，见善以相示也，爵位
相先也，患难相
死也，久相待也，
远祖致也。其任
举有如此者。

儒者中有这样的人：听到美好的言论便告诉他人，见到美好的行为便指示给他人；
Confucian scholars will tell other people about any good speeches they have heard. When they see some kind act, they will point to it so that others can see it as well.

受爵位则彼此相让，遇患难争相献身；
When the monarch grants them ranks of nobility, they will resign the higher ranks, saying that others deserve them more than they do. In the face of adversity, they will vie with others to sacrifice themselves first.

有朋友在下位，则等待他使之进用，朋友在远方则设法招来使其仕于君主。
When a friend is in a lower position, they will wait for him to get a promotion. When a friend is staying in a far-away place, they will lure him over so that he can work for the monarch.

儒者的任职和荐贤有这样做的。
Confucian scholars will hold public office and make recommendations like this.

仪表堂堂，是个人物。
He has a distinguished air.
He is somebody.

儒有澡身而浴德，陈言而伏，静而正之。上弗知也，粗而翘之，又不急为也。不临深而为高，不加少而为多。世治不轻，世乱不沮。同弗与，异弗非也。其特立独行有如此者。

儒者有这样的人：沐浴于道德以洁身，
Confucian scholars will bathe in morality to clean themselves.

铺陈意见而服侍君主，宁静而恪守正道，
They give wise counsel and suggestions to the monarch, remaining tranquil and keeping to the right course.

morality
道 德

国君不知道的事，则委婉进言，而不匆忙地去做。
They will tactfully tell a monarch things he doesn't know; they will not do things hurriedly without informing the monarch first.

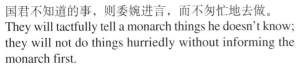

不在地位低下的人面前显示自己的高贵，不在功绩小的人面前显示自己的多能；
They will not flaunt their high position to people ranking below them. Nor will they brag about their abilities to people who have achieved less.

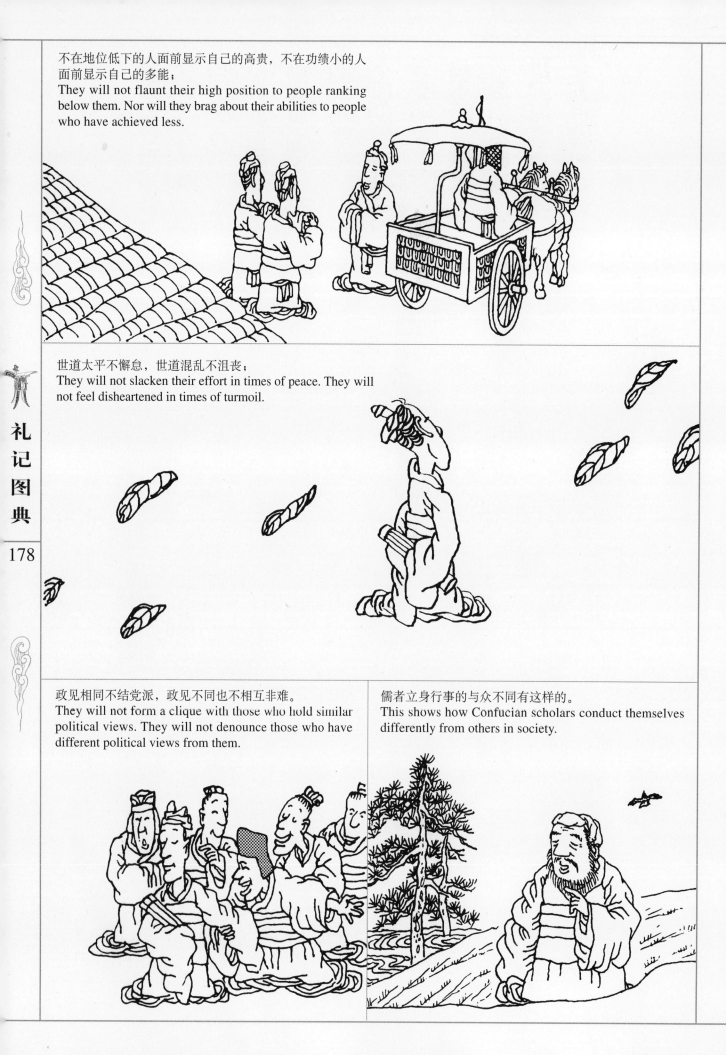

世道太平不懈怠，世道混乱不沮丧；
They will not slacken their effort in times of peace. They will not feel disheartened in times of turmoil.

政见相同不结党派，政见不同也不相互非难。
They will not form a clique with those who hold similar political views. They will not denounce those who have different political views from them.

儒者立身行事的与众不同有这样的。
This shows how Confucian scholars conduct themselves differently from others in society.

儒有上不臣天子，下不事诸侯。慎静而尚宽，强毅以与人，博学以知服。近文章，砥厉廉隅。虽分国如锱铢，不臣不仕。其规为有如此者。

儒者中有这样的人：上不做天子的臣下，下不为诸侯的吏属。谨慎恭敬而崇尚宽容，刚强坚毅而不随波逐流。

Some Confucian scholars refuse to serve as ministers of a monarch or subordinates of a prince. They are prudent, respectful and tolerant. They are resolute and never drift with the tide.

学识广博而力行使命，文质彬彬，仍不断磨励自己的气节。
They are erudite, sophisticated scholars who are devoted to their mission. They are always strengthening their moral integrity.

即使把国家分封与他，也被视为草芥，既不称臣，也不做官。儒者的行为规范有这样的。
They will regard estate allotted to them as trash. They refuse to serve as ministers in the imperial court or hold public posts. This is the criteria for their behavior.

我不在家。
I am not at home.

儒有合志同方，
营道同术。
并立则乐，
相下不厌。久不
相见，闻流
言不信。
其行本
方立义，同
而进，不
同而退。其交
友有如此者。

儒者有这样的人：朋友志同道合，行事有相同的见解，
Some Confucian scholars have friends who are of like mind. They see eye to eye on many things.

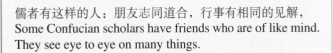

地位相等时相处和乐，地位悬殊时互不烦厌；
They have a friendly relationship when their social status is the same. They don't hate each other when there is a big difference between their positions.

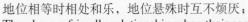

长久不见，听到有关朋友的谣言而不轻信，
When they haven't heard from each other for a long time, they will not give ready belief to rumors about their friend.

志向相同就一道前进，不同则自行避退。
When they and their friends share the same goals, they will advance together. When they don't, they will go separate ways.

儒者的交友原则有这样的。
This is the principle of Confucian scholars when they make friends.

温良者，仁之本也。敬慎者，仁之地也。宽裕者，仁之作也。孙接者，仁之能也。礼节者，仁之貌也。言谈者，仁之文也。歌乐者，仁之和也。分散者，仁之施也。儒皆兼此而有之，犹且不敢言仁也。其尊让有如此者。

温和善良是仁的根本；
Gentleness and kindness are the foundation of benevolence.

恭敬谨慎是仁的践履形式。
Deference and prudence are the form through which benevolence is practiced.

宽宏大量是仁的起始，
Magnanimity is the starting point of benevolence.

谦逊融洽是仁的功能。
Modesty and harmony are the functions of benevolence.

礼貌节仪是仁的表现，
Courtesy and rituals are the expression of benevolence.

言语谈论是仁的文饰，
Language and speech are the literary tools of benevolence.

"之乎者也" 的意义就在于此。
That's where the significance of zhi, hu, zhe, ye lies.

歌唱乐舞是仁的中和，
Singing and dancing are the harmony of benevolence.

分恩散物是仁的施与。
Charitable acts are the results of benevolence.

儒者兼有这些美德，尚不敢自以为便合乎仁的标准呢。
Even possessing all these virtues, Confucian scholars dare not say they are up to the standard of benevolence.

儒者的尊仁让善，有这样做的。
Confucian scholars did all this to show their deference, benevolence, magnanimity and kindness.

儒有不陨获于贫贱，不充诎于富贵。不慁君王，不累长上，不闵有司，故曰儒。今众人之命儒也妄。常以儒相诟病。孔子至舍，哀公馆之，闻此言也，言加信，行加义，终没吾世，不敢以儒为戏。

儒者有这样的人：不因为贫贱而坠落，不因为富贵而失节。
Confucian scholars will not resign themselves to degeneration because they are poor. They will not lose their integrity because they are rich or powerful.

请您将这段历史稍加更改。
Please make some changes to this history.

这人……
This man....

也不由于被天子、诸侯、卿大夫所困迫，便违背道义。所以称为"儒"。
They will not run counter to the norms of morality or justice because they are treated unfairly by emperors, dukes or ministers. Hence, they were given the name "Confucian scholar."

现在大家对儒者的看法都是荒唐的。
At present people's views about Confucian scholars are absurd.

常常以称他人为"儒"来相互诋毁。
They call a person "Confucian scholar" as a way to slander him.

这就是"儒"！
This is a Confucian scholar.

这是由于当时的很多人无儒者之行而为儒者之服、无儒者之实而盗儒者之名所致。
This is because people who are not Confucian scholars wear Confucian scholars' clothes and do bad things in the name of Confucian scholars.

儒者！
Confucian scholars.

儒！
Confucian scholars.

孔子回到馆舍，哀公招待他住下。听到上面的这些话后，谈话更讲信用，行为更合道理。
Duke Ai arranged for Confucius to stay in a guesthouse. After the talk with Confucius, Duke Ai's speech and actions were more trustworthy and sensible than before.

并且说："直到一生终了，再也不敢以'儒'来取笑他人了。"
Duke Ai said, "From now until I die, I will never again call a person 'Confucian scholar' to make fun of him."

月　令

月令，其中"月"指天文，"令"为政事。东汉经学家蔡邕说："古者诸侯朝正于天子，受月令以归，而藏诸庙中。天子藏之于明堂。每月告朔朝庙，出而行之。"全篇按十二个月的不同季节，规定了所必须从事的政治、生产、祭祀等方面的活动，实际上是设计了一套依天文而施政事的理想范本，是"天人合一"世界观的具体体现。

Astronomy-guided Political Program

Cai Yong (132-192), an expert in the study of Confucian classics, said, "In ancient times when dukes paid respects to the emperor, they would receive a copy of the political program from the emperor. When the duke returned to his feudal state, he kept the program in the temple. The emperor kept his copy in the Hall of Brightness. (The dukes) would visit the temple in the first day of every lunar month and undertake major activities according to the program." The program specified the political activities, production, sacrificial offerings and other such events to be undertaken in different seasons throughout the 12 months. It is an ideal plan for conducting administrative activities according to the movements of the celestial bodies and the change of seasons. It is the embodiment of the world outlook that man is an integral part of nature.

月令

孟春之月，日在
營室，昏參中，
旦尾中。其日
甲乙。其帝太皞
其神句芒。
其蟲鱗。
其音角，
律中太蔟。
其數八。
其味酸，其
臭羶。其
祀戶，祭先脾。

正月孟春，太阳的位置在周天二十八星宿的营室附近。入夜前参星出现在南方天中，破晓时尾宿出现在南方天中。
In the first month of spring, the position of the sun is near the shi constellation.* At dusk the shen constellation appears in the southern sky. At the break of dawn the wei constellation can be seen in the southern sky.

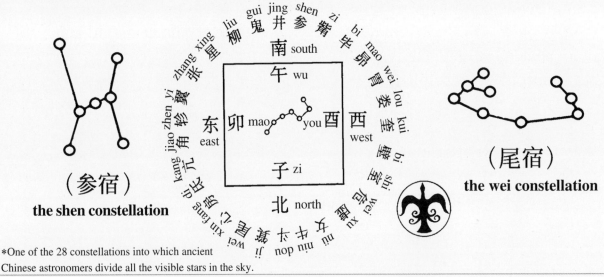

（参宿）
the shen constellation

（尾宿）
the wei constellation

*One of the 28 constellations into which ancient Chinese astronomers divide all the visible stars in the sky.

春之日为甲乙。在五行学说中，春在四季中属木，古人以十干记日，甲乙亦属木。
Spring days belong to jia and yi, Heavenly Stem one and two. According to the theory of the five elements, spring is wood. Ancient people use the ten Heavenly Stems to keep the dates. Jia and yi are wood by nature.

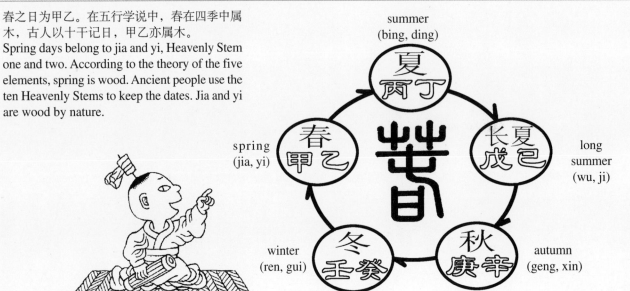

这时的主宰是木德之君的伏羲(太皞)；其神是少皞氏之子日重(苟芒)，属木官之臣。以二者为季节之神，是由于他们生前有功于民，其他四时之帝与神都是此义。动物以同样属木的鳞族为主。

The governing god of spring is Fuxi (Taihao), the king of wood virtue; the governing spirit is Rizhong (Goumang), the minister of wood. The two are regarded as the deities of spring because they conducted meritorious service to the people before they die. The deities of other seasons attained their status in similar fashion. Predominating animals in spring are animals with scales, which also belong to the category of wood.

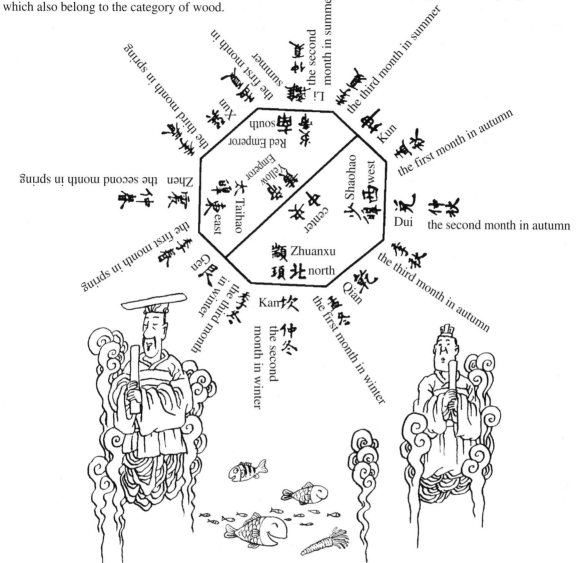

孟春与属木的角音相合。与十二律中的寅律太簇相应。

The first month of spring is compatible with the jue tone (one of the tones in the five-tone scale) which is wood by nature. It corresponds to the taicu tone in the 12-tone system.

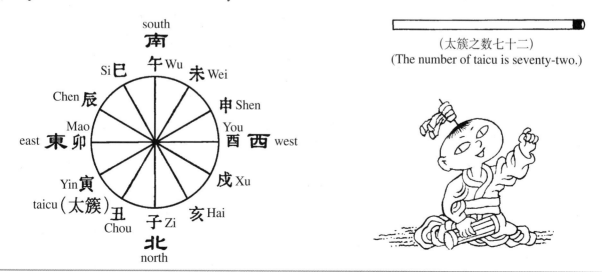

（太簇之数七十二）
(The number of taicu is seventy-two.)

律为校音之器，又为候气之管，古人以苇膜之灰堵其上口。根据阴阳之气，据地的深浅，依次埋于地中，据说其月气至，则灰飞而管通。为气之应。

Lü is an instrument for regulating musical tunes. The tubes also are used to test the energy flow from the earth. Ancient Chinese covered the upper openings of the tubes with a film made from reeds and buried the tubes under the ground. Every month the air from the inside the earth would blow away the thin film on the corresponding tubes.

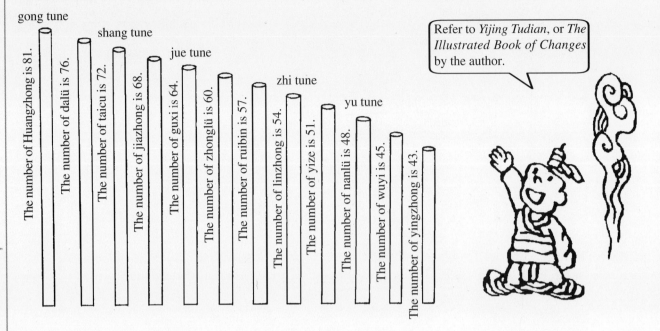

gong tune

The number of Huangzhong is 81.

shang tune

The number of dalü is 76.

The number of taicu is 72.

jue tune

The number of jiazhong is 68.

The number of guxi is 64.

The number of zhonglü is 60.

The number of ruibin is 57.

zhi tune

The number of linzhong is 54.

The number of yize is 51.

yu tune

The number of nanlü is 48.

The number of wuyi is 45.

The number of yingzhong is 43.

Refer to *Yijing Tudian*, or *The Illustrated Book of Changes* by the author.

数为土加木的"八"。为"天三生木"的成数，象征充满生机的春天。

The number reached by adding up the number of earth and wood is eight. It represents the vitality of spring.

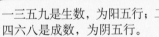

一三五九是生数，为阳五行；二四六八是成数，为阴五行。

One, three, five and nine are the original numbers and are yang by nature. Two, four, six and eight are the acquired numbers and are yin by nature.

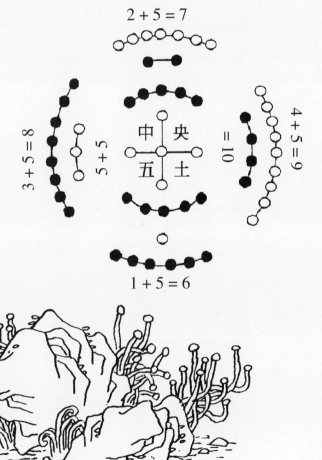

$2 + 5 = 7$

$3 + 5 = 8$

$5 + 5$

中央五土

$4 + 5 = 9$

$= 10$

$1 + 5 = 6$

口味是酸，气味为膻。
Your tongue can identify a vinegary taste and your nose the smell of mutton.

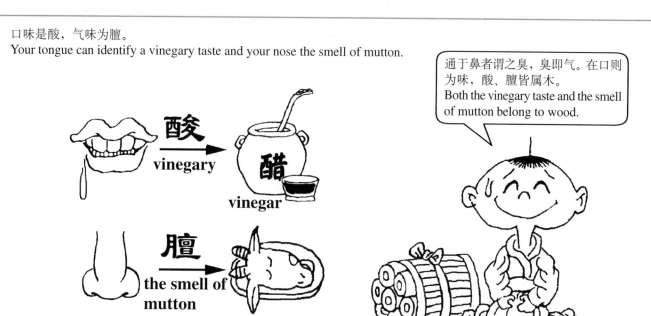

通于鼻者谓之臭，臭即气。在口则为味，酸、膻皆属木。
Both the vinegary taste and the smell of mutton belong to wood.

酸 vinegary
醋 vinegar
膻 the smell of mutton

《黄帝内经》之天门地户图
Chart of the Heavenly and Earthly Gates in the *Huangdi Neijing* (*Classic of Internal Medicine*)

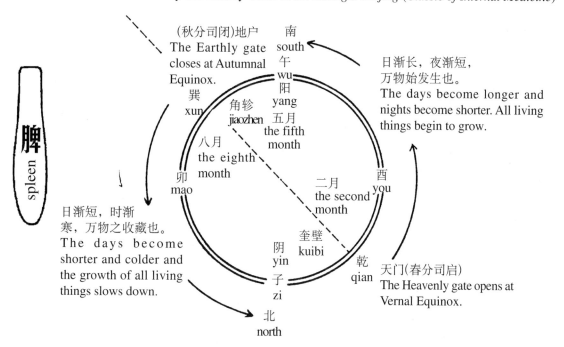

脾 spleen

(秋分司闭)地户
The Earthly gate closes at Autumnal Equinox.
巽 xun

角轸 jiaozhen

南 south
午 wu
阳 yang
五月 the fifth month

日渐长，夜渐短，万物始发生也。
The days become longer and nights become shorter. All living things begin to grow.

八月 the eighth month
卯 mao

二月 the second month

西 you

日渐短，时渐寒，万物之收藏也。
The days become shorter and colder and the growth of all living things slows down.

奎壁 kuibi
阴 yin
子 zi

乾 qian

天门(春分司启)
The Heavenly gate opens at Vernal Equinox.

北 north

"其祀户"的含义亦在于此。
That's why we should offer sacrifices to the god of the gate.

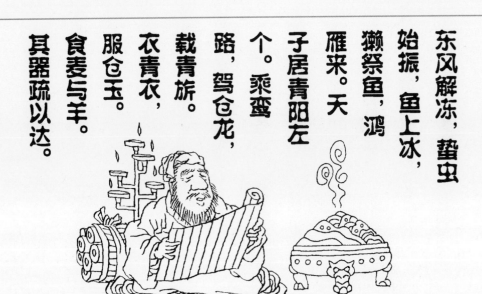

东风解冻，蛰虫始振，鱼上冰，獭祭鱼，鸿雁来。天子居青阳左个。乘鸾路，驾仓龙，载青旂。衣青衣，服仓玉。食麦与羊。其器疏以达。

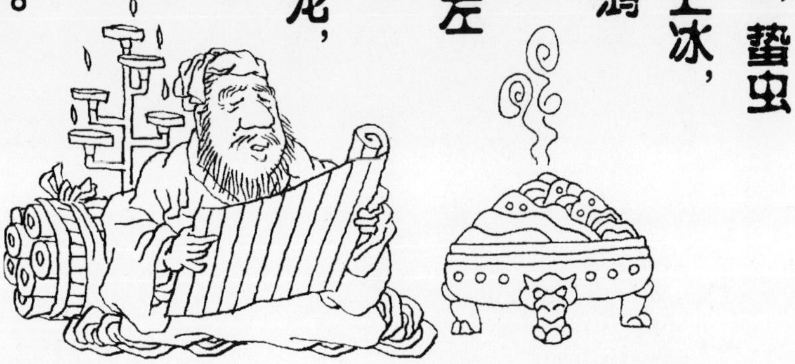

东风吹散严寒，蛰虫开始活动。
The easterly wind blows away the cold weather; insects that lie dormant in the soil during winter begin to stir.

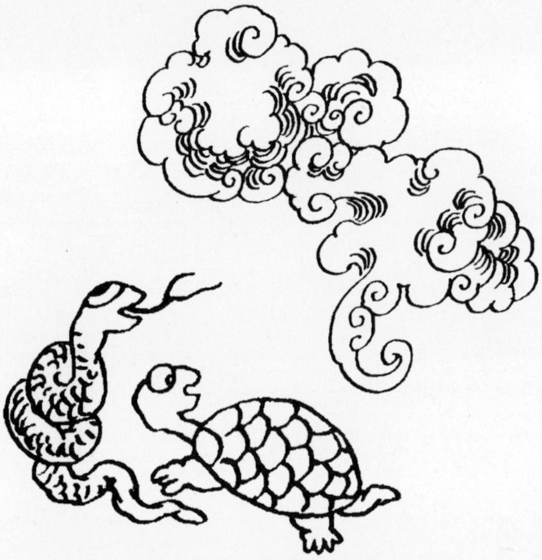

鱼游上近于冰。水獭临渊慕鱼。
Ice is beginning to thaw in the lakes and rivers. Fish swim to the surface of the water. An otter walks over to catch the fish.

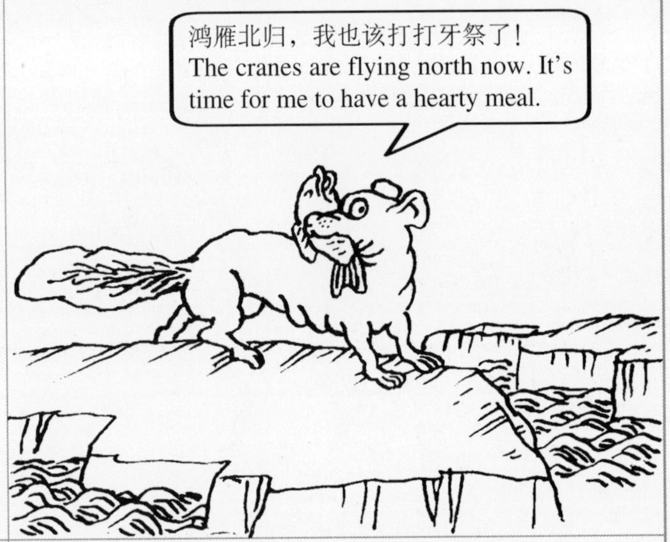
鸿雁北归，我也该打打牙祭了！
The cranes are flying north now. It's time for me to have a hearty meal.

天子居住在太寝东室偏北（东北）的左个（四面旁室谓“个”）。以与孟春之位相应。
To correspond to the first month of spring, the emperor stays in zuoge, the room in the northern part of the eastern chamber of the Taiqin Palace.

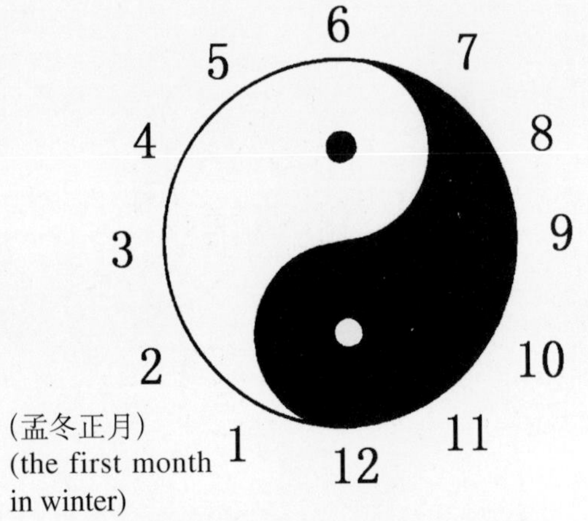
6
7
8
9
10
11
12
1
2
3
4
5
(孟冬正月)
(the first month in winter)

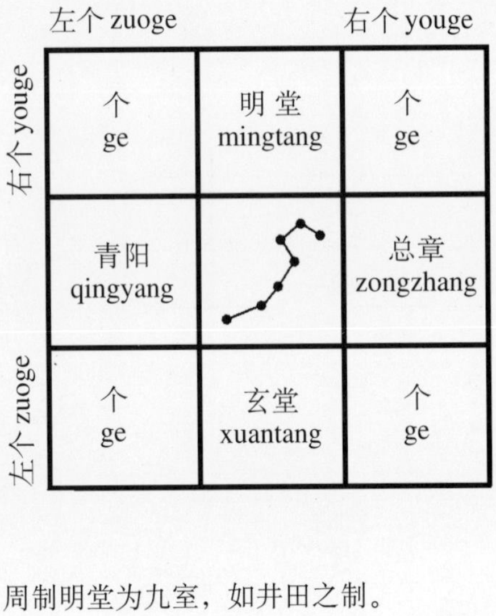
左个 zuoge
右个 youge
右个 youge
左个 zuoge
个 ge
明堂 mingtang
个 ge
青阳 qingyang
总章 zongzhang
个 ge
玄堂 xuantang
个 ge

按：周制明堂为九室，如井田之制。
Note: In the Zhou Dynasty (1100BC-221BC), the Hall of Brightness has nine rooms.

乘的是系有鸾铃的车子。驾的是八尺以上的苍龙之马，打着青色的旌旗。穿着青色的衣服，佩着青色的玉佩。
The emperor rides in a carriage pulled by horses eight feet tall flying green banners and adorned with bells in the shape of a legendary bird. The emperor wears green clothing and green jade pendant.

食物以麦和羊为主，麦与羊皆味苦。苦属火，取木生火之意，以提升体内阳气。
Wheat and sheep are their main source of food. Both have a bitter taste that is considered to belong to fire. By referring to the importance of starting a fire with wood, it intends to strengthen the yang energy in the human body.

用的器皿都要粗疏而与孟春的通透之气相应。
The utensils used are coarse so that the air of early spring can pass through.

是月也，以立春。
先立春三日，
太史谒之天子曰：
某日立春，盛
德在木。天子
乃齐。立春之日，
天子亲帅三公
九卿诸
侯大夫
以迎春于
东郊。还反，赏
公卿大夫于朝。

这个月，要定立春的节气。在立春之前三日，太史谒见天子，报告说："某日立春，为木德当令。"天子便开始斋戒。
During this month, the day that marks the beginning of spring is determined. Three days before the lichun, or Beginning of Spring, the Grand Astrologer will report to the emperor, "The Beginning of Spring is on such date. Things belonging to the element of wood are prospering." Then the emperor begins to fast.

立春之日，天子亲率众臣往东郊举行迎春之礼。礼毕归来，就在朝中
赏赐大家。
On the day of the Beginning of Spring, the emperor leads his ministers and officials to the eastern suburb to hold a ceremony to welcome spring. When the ceremony is over, they return to the imperial court where the emperor presents gifts to his officials.

命相布德和令，
行庆施惠，
下及兆民。庆
赐遂行，毋有
不当。乃
命太史
守典奉法，
司天日月星
辰之行，
宿离不贷，毋
失经纪，
以初为常。

命令三公发布恩德之令，褒扬善事，广施恩德，普及到万民。
The emperor orders the Minister of War, the Minister of Public Works and the Minister of Crime to promulgate a decree of royal favors. It sings the praise of good deeds and grants favors to a large number of ordinary people.

庆典布施依次进行，不得有误。
The ceremonies to praise the good and bestow favors are performed in exactly the right order without mistakes.

以此为占候之常。继而命令太史，根据观测天文的法典和技术，推算日月星辰的运行，务使它们运行的位置、度数与轨道，没有一步偏差，与历年的推算相同。
The emperor then orders the Grand Astrologer to calculate the movements of the sun, the moon and stars with the help of books and technologies used for making observations of celestial bodies to make sure the position, degree and orbit of their movements are exactly the same as the figures of previous years.

是月也，天子乃以元日祈谷于上帝。乃择元辰，天子亲载耒耜，措之于参保介之御间。帅三公、九卿、诸侯、大夫躬耕帝籍。天子三推，三公五推，卿诸侯九推。反，执爵于太寝，三公、九卿、诸侯、大夫皆御，命曰劳酒。

在这个月，天子在第一个辛日，祭祀上帝，祈祷丰收。
On the first xin day of this month, the emperor offers sacrifices to God, praying for a bumper harvest.

在亥日，天子亲自载着耒耜，放在卫士与御者之间。率领三公、九卿、诸侯、大夫，亲自在君主名下的田里耕作。
On the hai day, the emperor, with a plow in hand, leads his ministers, senior officials and dukes to work on a farmland under his name.

天子推三下，三公各推五下，卿和诸侯各推九下。
The emperor pushes the plow three times; the Minister of War, the Minister of Public Works and the Minister of Crime each push the plow five times. The dukes and other officials each push the plow nine times.

礼毕返回。天子在大寝殿举行宴会，三公、九卿、诸侯、大夫全部参加，称为"劳酒"。
After the ceremony they return to the imperial palace. The emperor gives a banquet in the Daqin Hall, attended by all the ministers, senior officials and dukes. It is called laojiu, or the "liquor for labor."

是月也，天气下降。地气上腾，天地合同，草木萌动。王命布农事，命田舍东郊，皆修封疆，审端径术。善相丘陵、阪险、原隰、土地所宜，五谷所植，以教道民。必躬亲之。田事既饬，先定准直，农事不惑。

这一月，天气下降，地气上升，天地之气交合，草木开始抽芽。
During this month, the heavenly air goes down and the earthly air comes up. They meet and mix and the grass and trees begin to sprout.

天子于是发布农事的命令。派遣官员住在东郊，把耕地的疆界全部修理起来，把小渠和小径整治端正。
The emperor gives orders for agricultural production. He dispatches officials to stay in the eastern suburbs. Under their supervision, the peasants put up posts to mark the borders between the farmland, clear the irrigation ditches and construct paths.

妥善地斟酌高地与低地适宜种植的作物，并将各种农作物的培植方法一一教会百姓，要求负责官员要亲自到场。
The officials in charge of agriculture ponder carefully which crops are suitable for highland farming and which are suitable for lowland farming. Then they go to the farmland to teach the peasants the cultivating method of each crop.

田地都已清理齐备，则预先制定好各项标准。
By the time the land is ready to be cultivated, the government has worked out the necessary criteria for the farming procedures and methods.

农民有了这些标准，才不至于迷乱。
With the criteria in place, peasants will understand what to do and how to do it.

是月也，命乐正入学习舞。乃修祭典，命祀山林川泽，牺牲毋用牝。禁止伐木。毋覆巢，毋杀孩虫、胎、夭、飞鸟，毋麛，毋卵。毋聚大众，毋置城郭。掩骼埋胔。

这个月，命乐正进入国学教练舞蹈。
During this month the emperor orders the dance master to teach dancing in the imperial college.

修订一年祭祀的典则。
The provisions and rules governing sacrificial offerings are revised.

命令祭祀山林川泽，牺牲不可用雌性的。
The emperor gives an order to offer sacrifices to the deities of mountains, forests and rivers, forbidding the use of female animals.

禁止砍伐树木。不许捣毁鸟巢。
Felling trees and destroying bird nests are strictly prohibited.

不包括它！
Not including this.

不许捕杀幼兽，不许掏取鸟卵。
Hunting and killing young animals is prohibited;
taking birds' eggs is prohibited.

不许残害幼虫、未出生的小兽、刚学飞的小鸟。
People are prohibited from harming larvae or animals which
are soon to be born or birds that are learning to fly.

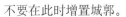

不许在这个月聚合群众，影响生产。
It is prohibited to gather crowds to hinder production.

不要在此时增置城郭。
The city wall must not be constructed at this time.

有枯骨腐肉都要埋掉。
Bury dry bones or rotten meat whenever you find them.

是月也不可以称兵。
称兵必天殃。
兵戎不起，不
可从我始。
毋变天之道，
毋绝地之理，毋
乱人之纪。

这个月，不可举兵征伐，举兵者必遭天殃。
It is not the right time to go on a punitive expedition this month. Those who do will be punished by Heaven.

不可发动战争，尤其是主动挑起战争。
Do not go to war. It is particularly bad to start a war.

干活儿去！
Go and do your work.

不可违背天的规律。
Do not go against the rules of heaven.

不可断绝地的道理(要依农时而作)。
Do not oppose the truths of earth (do farm work in accordance with the farming season).

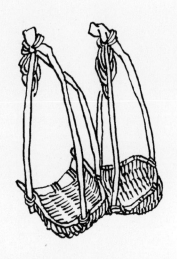

不要混乱人的纲纪。
Do not violate the customs of society.

仲春之月，日在奎。昏弧中，旦建星中。其日甲乙。其帝太皞，其神句芒。其虫鳞。其音角，律中夹钟。其数八。其味酸，其臭膻。其祀户。祭先脾。始雨水，桃始华。仓庚鸣。鹰化为鸠。

二月仲春，太阳行至奎宿附近，黄昏时井宿旁的弧星出现在南方天空。

In the second month of spring, the sun moves to the kui constellation. At dusk the lone star near the jing constellation appears in the southern sky.

破晓时斗宿旁的建星出现在南方天中。

At the break of dawn, the star jian near the dou constellation appears in the southern sky.

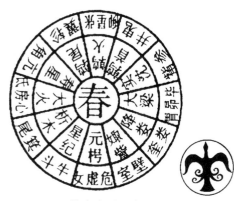

仲春之月
the second month of spring

建星
the star *jian*

斗宿
the *dou* constellation

这一月与十二律中的卯律夹钟相应。天上开始下雨，桃树开始开花，黄鹂鸣啭，苍鹰隐去，布谷鸟出现在田野。

This month corresponds to the jiazhong tone in the 12-tone system. It begins to rain; peach trees bloom. Orioles chirp but goshawks have vanished. Cuckoos appear in the fields.

(夹钟) 卯 (jiazhong) mao

si 巳　wu 午　wei 未
辰 chen　　　shen 申
　　　　　　　you 酉
　　　　　　　xu 戌
寅 yin　　　亥 hai
丑 chou　子 zi

天子居青阳太庙。乘鸾路，驾仓龙，载青旂。衣青衣，服仓玉。食麦与羊。其器疏以达。

是月也，安萌芽，养幼少，存诸孤。择元日，命民社。命有司省囹圄，去桎梏，毋肆掠，止狱讼。

这个月天子移居到青阳太庙的东堂。
This month, the emperor moves to stay in the eastern quarters of the Qingyang imperial ancestral temple.

此时生物刚开始萌发，要保养幼小者。抚恤遗族子弟。
This is the time when living things are beginning to grow. Take care of the young. Comfort and give compensation to orphans.

选择甲日这天，使百姓举行社祭。
On the jia day, ordinary people offer sacrifices to the god of land.

让司法官减少拘系的囚徒，除去脚镣手铐，不许搜刮民财，停止民事诉讼。
Court officials are required to reduce the number of prisoners in jail and remove the shackles and handcuffs from the prisoners. It is forbidden to fleece the people. Stop all civil lawsuits.

这个月，燕子归来。归来之日，就用牛羊猪三牲礼拜高贵的禖神，以祈嗣。
Swallows return during this month. On the day when a swallow flies back, cows, sheep, and pigs should be presented to the god of fertility to pray for offspring.

是月也，玄鸟至。至之日，以太牢祠于高禖，天子亲往，后妃帅九嫔御。乃礼天子所御，带以弓韣，授以弓矢，于高禖之前。

天子亲自参加，后妃率领全体后宫也同去。
The emperor will take part in such a ceremony accompanied by the empress and all his concubines in the imperial harem.

要向受孕的后妃行礼，让她们带着弓套，交给她们弓箭，这些都于高贵的禖神前举行。
In front of the god of fertility, the other concubines will salute the pregnant concubines who hold the sheaths while they are presented with bows and arrows.

是月也，日夜分，雷乃发声，始电。蛰虫咸动，启户始出。先雷三日，奋木铎以令兆民曰：雷将发声，有不戒其容止者，生子不备，必有凶灾！日夜分，则同度量，钧衡石，角斗甬，正权概。

这个月，白天和黑夜的时刻渐渐持平，可听到打雷，开始闪电。
In this month, the length of day and night gradually becomes the same. One can hear thunder and lightning.

蛰虫开始蠕动，从土洞中爬出。
Insects that lie dormant in the soil during winter begin to crawl out of their underground shelters.

在春分的前三日，要使人摇动着木铎，警告天下万民说："快要打雷了，大家的私生活要检点。不然将会生下有残疾的孩子，父母也要遭残。"

Three days before Vernal Equinox, the government will dispatch men who shake wooden bells while shouting out warnings, "There will be thunder soon. Everyone should restrain themselves in their private lives. Otherwise, you will give birth to handicapped children. Parents will suffer deformities as well."

在日夜平分的日子，可以统一度量，平均衡石，校正斗甬，纠正枰锤、手尺。

On the day when day and night have equal length, we will unify the measures. All weights, dou measures, scales and rulers must be rectified.

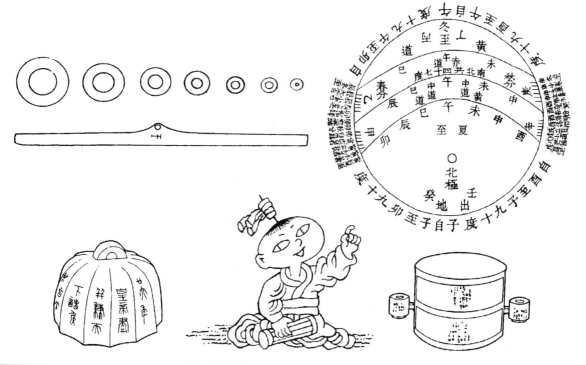

是月也，耕者少舍，乃修阖扇，寝庙毕备。

毋作大事，以妨农之事。

是月也，毋竭川泽，毋漉陂池，毋焚山林。

天子乃鲜羔开冰，先荐寝庙。

上丁，命乐正习舞释菜。天子乃帅三公九卿诸侯大夫亲往视之。仲丁又命乐正入学习乐。

是月也，祀不用牺牲，用圭璧，更皮币。

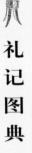

这个月，农人们稍得空闲，便在此时修理门窗户扇，使前堂和后室齐备完整。
During this month, peasants will take time to repair the doors and windows of their houses so that they are in good condition.

这个月，不可戽干河川湖泊的水，不要用网在陂池中捕鱼。
During this month, people should not drain rivers or lakes. They must not use nets to catch fish in the pond.

不要兴兵打仗，那样会妨碍农事。
We should not go to war, because it will interrupt agricultural production.

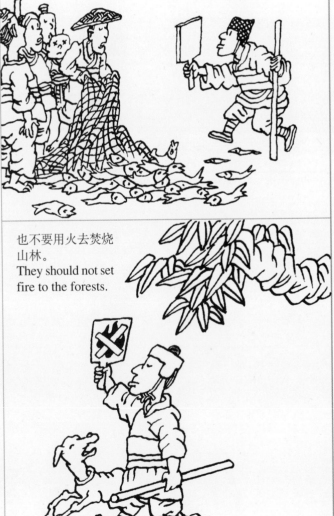

也不要用火去焚烧山林。
They should not set fire to the forests.

然后，君主奉献小羊和从冰窖中取来的冰，先在寝庙中举行荐礼。
Then the emperor holds a ceremony in the ancestral temple to offer lamb and ice (which he gets from an icehouse) to his ancestors.

在第一个丁日，命乐正前往国学教习舞蹈，并以释菜之礼祭祀先师。
On the first ding day, the emperor orders his chief musician to teach dancing in the imperial college and hold a sacrificial offering ceremony to honor the former masters.

天子亲自率领三公九卿诸大夫，前往视察。
The emperor leads his ministers and senior officials to the imperial college for inspection.

第二个丁日，又命令乐正往国学里练习乐舞。这个月，祭祀一般不用牺牲，改用圭璧，规模再小些的祭祀则以皮币代替。
On the second ding day, the emperor orders his chief musician to supervise the playing of music and dancing in the imperial college. In this month they don't use animals as sacrificial offerings to the gods or ancestors. Instead, they use jade tablets for major ceremonies and cloth, silk or pelt for minor ones.

圭   璧

季春之月，日在胃，昏七星中，旦牵牛中。其日甲乙。其帝太皥，其神句芒。其虫鳞。其音角，律中姑洗。其数八。其味酸，其臭膻。其祀户，祭先脾。桐始华，田鼠化为鴽，虹始见。萍始生。

三月季春，太阳行到在二十八宿中的胃宿，黄昏时可看到星宿在南方天中。黎明时牛宿在南方天中。

In the third month of spring, the sun moves to the wei constellation. At dusk one can see the xing constellation in the southern sky; at the break of dawn one can see the niu constellation in the southern sky.

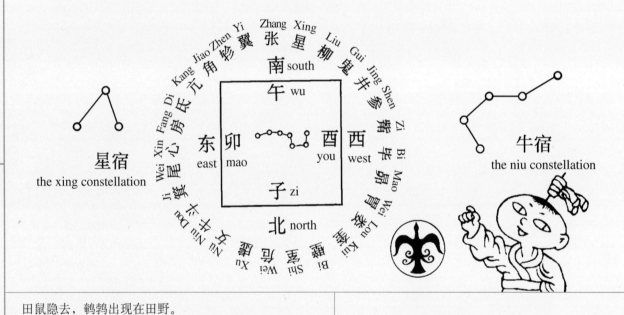

星宿
the xing constellation

南 south
午 wu
东 卯 east mao
酉 you 西 west
子 zi
北 north

牛宿
the niu constellation

田鼠隐去，鹌鹑出现在田野。
Field rodents have vanished; quails appear in the field.

还有我们呢!
Don't forget us.

彩虹开始出现，浮萍开始生长。
Rainbows often appear in the sky; duckweed begins to grow.

天子居青阳右个。
乘鸾路，驾
仓龙，载青旂。
衣青衣，
服仓玉。
食麦与羊。
其器疏以达。
是月也，
天子乃荐
鞠衣于先帝。
命舟牧覆舟，
五覆五反，
乃告舟备具于
天子焉。天子
始乘舟。荐鲔于
寝庙，乃为麦祈实。

这个月，天子移居到青阳宫殿的右个。用桑始生之色的礼服祭祀先帝，以祈祷蚕茧丰收。

In this month, the emperor moves to stay in the youge chamber in the Qingyang Palace. He offers to the late king a ceremonial robe that is the color of the young leaves of a mulberry tree, praying for a harvest of silkworm cocoon.

命主管船只者检查船只，将船面船底反复检查五次。没有疏漏，才报告给君主，君主开始乘船。

By order of the emperor the person in charge of boats checks the boat five times before reporting to the emperor that the boat is in perfect condition. Then the emperor gets on the boat.

用小鱼在寝庙中祭祀，并祈祷小麦丰收。

In the state temple, the emperor offers small fish as sacrifices to gods and ancestors, praying for a bumper harvest of wheat.

是月也，生气方盛，阳气发泄，句者毕出，萌者尽达，不可以内。天子布德行惠，命有司发仓廪，赐贫穷，振乏绝；开府库，出币帛，周天下；勉诸侯，聘名士，礼贤者。

这个月，生气最盛，阳气舒朗。卷曲的嫩芽尽出，芒尖的萌芽也都舒展开来。

Things are full of vitality this month. The yang energy is mild. The tender buds have blossomed.

这时不可以吝啬闭藏。天子应布德施恩，接济百姓。

Wealthy people should be generous this month. The emperor should grant favors to the ordinary people.

命主管官员打开粮仓赠粮食给贫苦者。

The emperor orders his officials to open the granaries to distribute grain among the poor.

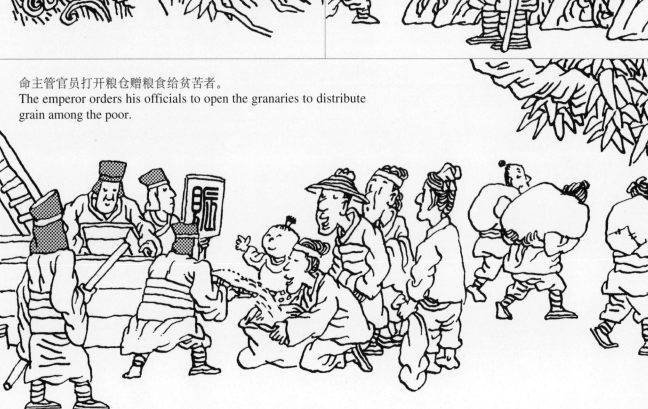

赈济那些缺衣少食、三餐不继的人们。
They provide food to those who need it badly.

又叫政府破费了！
I am grateful to the government.

打开府库，拿出币帛，普施天下。
They also take cloth and silk from the warehouses and give them to the people.

勉励诸侯，礼聘才德兼备的学者贤士。
The emperor praises the dukes and princes and cordially enlists the service of virtuous and capable scholars and officials.

礼记图典

211

是月也，命司空曰：「時雨將降，下水上騰。循行國邑，周視原野，修利堤防，道達溝瀆，開通道路，毋有障塞。田獵置罘，羅、網、畢、翳、餧獸之藥，毋出九門。」

这个月，命令司空说："雨季即将来到，地下水开始上涌，赶快巡视国内各地，遍察大地的情形。"
The emperor gives orders to the Minister of Territorial Resources, "The rainy season is coming. The subterranean water will flow upward. Inspect the country immediately to investigate the situation of all the regions."

"必须修好要修整的堤防，立即疏导淤塞的沟渠。开通道路，去除障碍。"
"It is essential to construct embankments, dredge the ditches, open up roads and remove all obstacles."

"擒捕鸟兽用的器具和毒害鸟兽用的药物，一概不许携带出城中九门。"
"Implements that are used to catch birds and animals, poison that is used to kill birds and animals are not allowed to be carried out of the nine city gates."

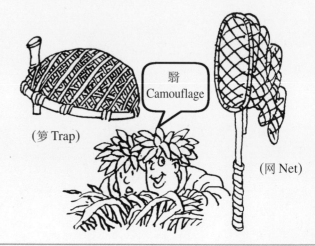

（笭 Trap）

翳
Camouflage

（网 Net）

礼记图典

212

是月也，命野虞毋伐桑柘。鸣鸠拂其羽，戴胜降于桑，具曲植蘧筐。后妃齐戒，亲东乡躬桑，禁妇女毋观，省妇使，以劝蚕事。蚕事既登，分茧称丝效功，以共郊庙之服，毋有敢惰。

这个月，命令看守山林田野的官员，禁止任何人砍伐桑树枝干。
In this month, officials in charge of forests and the fields are ordered to prohibit people from cutting off the boughs of mulberry trees.

斑鸠拍打翅膀，戴胜起落于桑林之间，这时就要准备好养蚕的木架和薄筐。
Turtledoves flap their wings. Hoopoe rise up from the mulberry forest and then fly back. It is time to get the wooden support and bamboo pan ready for rearing silkworms.

蘧
circular bamboo pan

筐
square bamboo pan

天子的后妃斋戒后，迎着时气，亲自到东乡动手采桑。
After fasting the queen and the royal concubines go to Dongxiang to pick mulberry leaves.

禁止妇女们过分妆扮，减少她们的杂务，使之专心饲蚕。
Women are prohibited from spending too much time dressing themselves up. Their chores are reduced so that they can concentrate on rearing the silkworms.

待到蚕事完成，就分派蚕茧给大家抽丝，然后称量轻重来看其成绩。
After all the silkworms have spun cocoons, the people reel off raw silk from the cocoons. Then the raw silk is weighed to see how efficient they were.

用此蚕丝制成祭天的礼服，不许怠惰。
Ceremonial robes worn by people when offering sacrifices to gods are made with the silk.

是月也，命工
师令百工审五库
之量：金铁、
皮革筋、角齿、
羽箭干、脂胶
丹漆，毋
或不良。百
工咸理，
监工日号：
毋悖于时，
毋或作为
淫巧以荡上心！

这个月，命令工师使百工查验五库的储藏，金铁、皮革筋、角齿、羽箭干、脂胶丹漆，都要质地良好的。
In this month, craftsmen are ordered to check the following goods stored in the Five Warehouses: Gold, iron, leather, animal horns, arrow shafts, resin and pigment to make sure they are of good quality.

然后各类匠人从事制作，监工每日发出号令督促大家。要按制造程序，
不要违背时限。
Then the craftsmen begin to work. Foremen give them orders to supervise their work. They make things according to procedures that do not violate the season.

在"天人合一"的背景下，古人制作物品都有一定的时序。
Guided by the theory that "man is an integral part of nature," ancient people made different things in different times of the year.
以弓为例："必春液角，夏治筋，秋合三材。"
Take the bow for example. "Wood was bent in spring, string was made in summer and the different parts were put together in autumn."

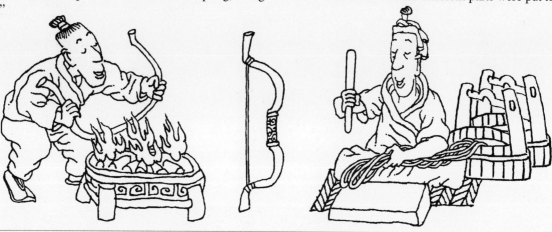

加之工匠对自然的敬畏与虔诚，器物由此融入了天地四时之气。
Because the craftsmen showed reverence for nature, the tools they made were infused with the vital energy of heaven, the earth and the four seasons.

与自然的结合到了这种自觉的地步，器物自然神完气足了。
The combination with nature reached such a seamless level that the tools fashioned were of high quality.

再就是不要制作过于奇巧的东西，来扰动君主心性！
Do not make strange gadgets to distract the mind of the monarch.

人应自觉地效法自然，而无出其外。
People should consciously follow the rules of nature and not deviate from them.

请看。
Look at this.

是月之末，择吉日，大合乐，天子乃率三公九卿诸侯大夫往视之。是月也，乃合累牛腾马，游牝于牧。牺牲驹犊，举书其数。命国难，九门磔攘，以毕春气。

这个月，择定吉日，举行盛大舞会，天子率领三公、九卿、诸侯、大夫亲自前往参观。
A grand party is held during the month on a day that has been considered auspicious. The emperor takes his ministers, princes and senior officials to the party.

这个月春阳既盛，是产育的开始，于是聚合累系之牛(良种牛)、腾跃之马(良种马)，把它们放养到牧场上，使其交配繁衍。

In this month, the spring yang energy is thriving; it is the beginning of propagation. Ox and stallions are put out to the pasture to mate and breed.

祭祀所用小牛小马，生下后都要及时记录其数量。
The number of calves and foals to be used as sacrifices will be recorded as soon as they are born.

命全国举行除祸驱疫的傩祭，在九门分食供品，来结束春的节气。
Orders are given to practice exorcism all over the country to expel evil spirits and plague. At Jiumen, people eat the offerings to bring an end to the spring season.

礼记图典

218

孟夏之月，日在毕。昏翼中，旦婺女中。其日丙丁。其帝炎帝，其神祝融。其虫羽。其音徵，律中中吕。其数七。其味苦，其臭焦。其祀灶，祭先肺。

四月孟夏，太阳行至在二十八宿的毕宿附近，黄昏时翼宿出现在南方的天中。

In the first month in summer, the sun moves to the bi constellation. At dusk one can see the yi constellation in the southern sky.

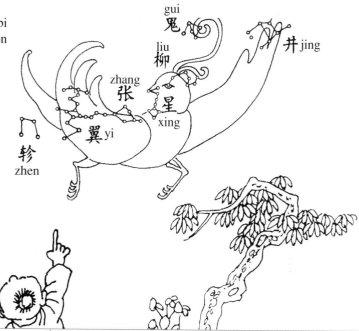

清晨女宿出现在南方天中。

At dawn, the nü constellation appears in the southern sky.

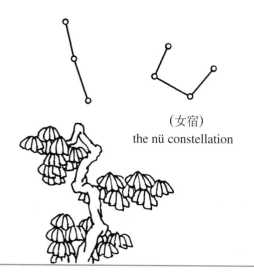

（女宿）
the nü constellation

日为丙丁。夏在四季中属火，在记日的十干中，丙丁亦属火。

The sun belongs to bing and ding, the third and fourth Heavenly Stems. According to the theory of the five elements, the essence of summer is fire. Ancient people used the Heavenly Stems to keep the date; bing and ding are also fire by nature.

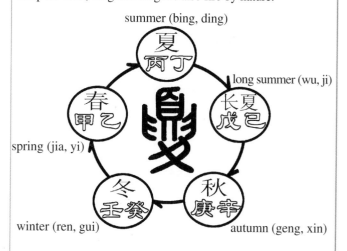

summer (bing, ding)
long summer (wu, ji)
spring (jia, yi)
autumn (geng, xin)
winter (ren, gui)

礼记图典

219

主宰该季节的大帝是赤精之君，炎帝神农。
The ruling king of this season is the Yandi, or the Red Emperor.

其神为颛顼之子，火官之臣祝融。
The governing deity is Zhu Rong.

炎帝
Yandi

祝融
Zhu Rong

夏季所繁育的动物为属火的飞鸟。
Animals bred in summer and birds with plumage are fire by nature.

五音合于属火的徵，与十二律的巳律仲吕相应。
This month is compatible with the zhi tone (one of the tones in the five-tone scale) which is fire by nature. It corresponds to the zhonglü tone in the 12-tone system.

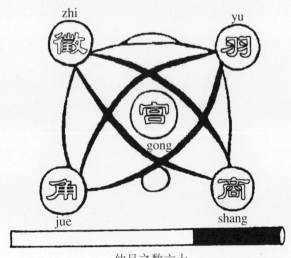

zhi
yu
gong
jue
shang

仲吕之数六十
The number of zhonglü is 60.

其数是土加火的七，为地二生火的成数。
The number is seven—the sum of earth (five) and fire (two).

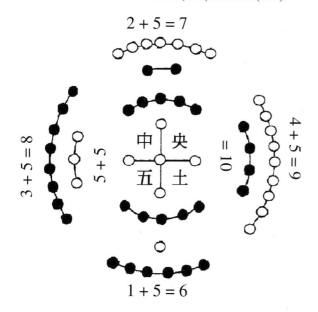

2 + 5 = 7

3 + 5 = 8

5 + 5

中央
五土

= 10

4 + 5 = 9

1 + 5 = 6

口味是苦的，气味是焦的，苦与焦，均属火。
The predominant smell of this month is the bitter, burnt smell. They are fire in essence.

祭祀的对象是灶，因为灶以火养人。
People offer sacrifices to the kitchen range because the fire in the kitchen range helps people survive.
祭品以肺为上，是由于肺属金，而火可克金。
The best sacrificial item is the lung which is metal by nature. According to the theory of the five elements, fire subdues metal.

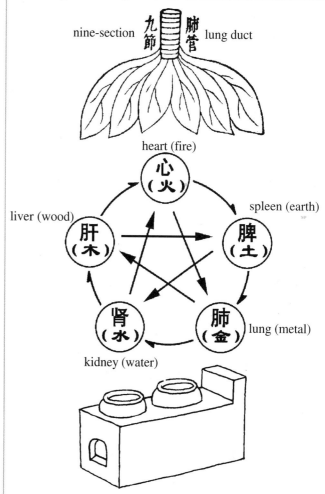

nine-section 九節 肺管 lung duct

heart (fire)
心（火）

spleen (earth)
脾（土）

liver (wood)
肝（木）

lung (metal)
肺（金）

kidney (water)
肾（水）

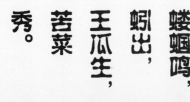

蝼蝈鸣，蚯
蚓出，
王瓜生，
苦菜
秀。

巳月之候为：蛤蟆鸣叫。
In this month toads croak.

蚯蚓出土。
Earthworms come out from under the earth.

栝楼结实。苦菜长大。
Chinese trichosanthes bear fruit; common sow thistle grows.

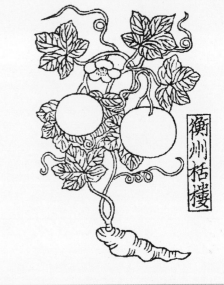

衡州栝楼

王瓜色赤，感火之色而生。
Chinese trichosanthes are red because they are influenced by fire.

苦菜味苦，感火之味而成。
Common sow thistle is bitter because it is influenced by fire.

天子居明堂
左个；，
乘朱路，
驾赤骝 载
赤旂；，衣朱
衣，服赤玉；，
食菽与
鸡。其器
高以粗。

天子移居到明堂左个，乘红色的车，驾红色的马，载红色的旗，着红色的衣，佩红色的玉。
The emperor moves to stay in the zuoge of the Hall of Brightness. He rides in a red carriage pulled by red horses with red banners. The emperor wears red clothes and red jade.

用的器皿是高而粗大的，体现物在这一季节的苗壮。
The utensils used are tall and rough, indicating that things are prospering during the season.

食品以豆实和鸡为主。
Food, during this month, consists mostly of beans and chicken.

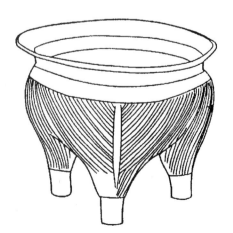

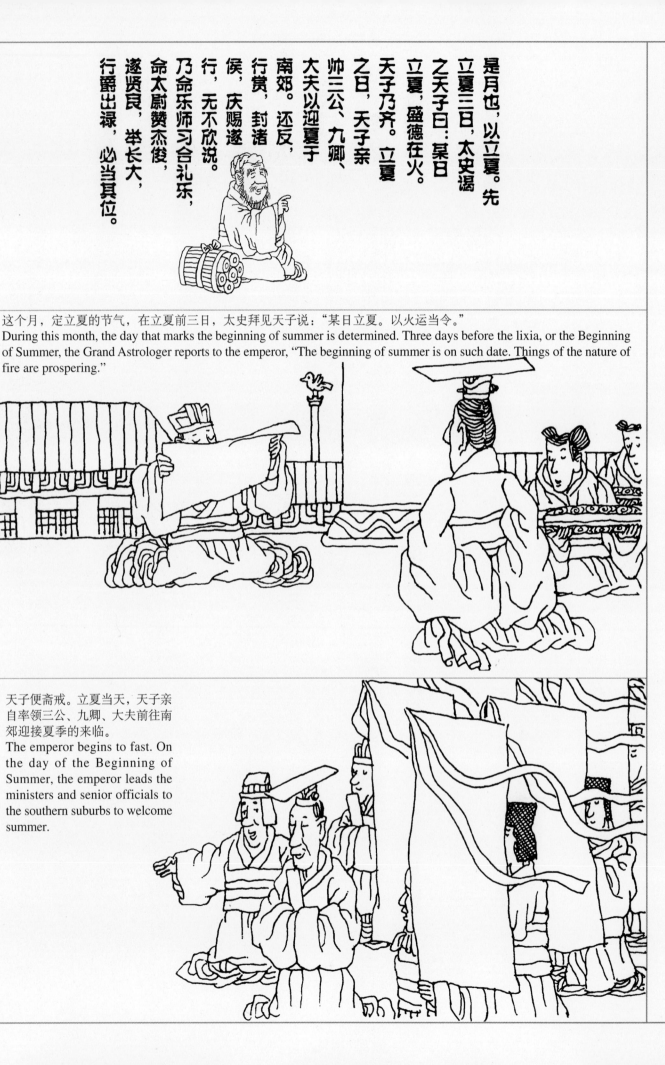

是月也，以立夏。先立夏三日，太史谒之天子曰：某日立夏，盛德在火。天子乃齐。立夏之日，天子亲帅三公、九卿、大夫以迎夏于南郊。还反，行赏，封诸侯，庆赐遂行，无不欣说。乃命乐师习合礼乐，命太尉赞杰俊，遂贤良，举长大，行爵出禄，必当其位。

这个月，定立夏的节气，在立夏前三日，太史拜见天子说："某日立夏。以火运当令。"

During this month, the day that marks the beginning of summer is determined. Three days before the lixia, or the Beginning of Summer, the Grand Astrologer reports to the emperor, "The beginning of summer is on such date. Things of the nature of fire are prospering."

天子便斋戒。立夏当天，天子亲自率领三公、九卿、大夫前往南郊迎接夏季的来临。

The emperor begins to fast. On the day of the Beginning of Summer, the emperor leads the ministers and senior officials to the southern suburbs to welcome summer.

礼毕归来，就大行赏赐，分封诸侯人等，庆典与赏赐依次进行，大众无不欢悦。

After the welcoming ceremony the emperor showers the princes, ministers and officials with gifts. Everyone is happy.

于是命乐师演习礼乐。

The emperor orders the royal musicians to perform the ritual music.

又命太尉表彰德才兼备者，让贤良者受人仰慕。

He orders the Defender-in-Chief to commend the virtuous and capable people, who become the admiration of the general public.

再执技论力，选拔魁梧高大者，予以任用。

A competition is held to select people who are strong and powerful to work for the government.

依据爵位授以俸禄，使人才爵禄配合恰当。

Salaries are paid according to the ranks of nobility so that they correspond with an individual's abilities.

是月也，继长增高，毋有坏堕。毋起土功，毋发大众，毋伐大树。是月也，天子始绨。命野虞出行田原，为天子劳农劝民，毋或失时。命司徒巡行县鄙，命农勉作，毋休于都。是月也，驱兽毋害五谷，毋大田猎。

这一月，一切生物都在生长增高，不要有毁坏的行为伤害作物已成之气。
In this month, all living things are growing up; people shouldn't do anything to destroy them.

不要举行大的土木工程，不要征集大众，以妨蚕农之事。
Do not recruit laborers for large-scale civil engineering projects because doing so will disrupt sericulture.

不要砍伐大树。
Do not cut down big trees.

这个月，天子开始换上夏日的衣服。
The emperor wears summer clothing during this month.

命令主管田野山林的官员到各地，代表天子慰劳农民，勉励其生产，不可错过农作的季节。
On behalf of the emperor, officials in charge of agriculture and forestry will convey greetings to the farmers and give them gifts, encouraging them to do well in production and not let the farming season pass by.

命令司徒到县鄙巡视，让各地的农官认真指导，不要停留在都市中。
The emperor tells the Minister of Land and People to go on an inspection of the remote areas to ask officials in charge of agriculture not to stay in the cities but to go to the countryside to give farmers instructions on production.

这一月，要经常驱赶野兽，不使它们伤害五谷。
In this month, people will scare away the birds so that they will not damage the food crops.

但不可举行大规模的田猎。
Large-scale hunting is forbidden.

农乃登麦。天子乃
以彘尝麦，先荐
寝庙。是月也。
聚畜百药。靡草死，
麦秋至。断
薄刑，决小罪，
出轻系。
蚕事毕，
后妃献茧，乃
收茧税，以桑
为均，贵贱长
幼如一，以给郊庙
之服。是月也，天
子饮酎，用礼乐。

农官献上新麦，天子便用猪配合行尝麦之礼，先献于寝庙。
The agricultural official presents new ears of wheat. The emperor holds a ceremony featuring a pig tasting the wheat and dedicates them to the ancestral temple.

这个月，要积蓄各种药物。
People store up all kinds of medicines during this month.

这时荠菜等枝叶靡细的植物已经枯萎，到了麦子成熟的季节。
Plants with thin branches and leaves like shepherd's purse have withered. It is the season when wheat is ripe.

凡是判以轻微体罚的，罪行不太严重的，短期拘禁的，判决后都应释放。

Those who have been sentenced to light corporal punishment or short-term detainment, and those who commit minor offences will be released after the sentence is announced.

饲蚕的工作已经结束，后妃们举行献茧之礼。

The work to raise silkworms has now come to an end. The empress and the imperial concubines will hold a ceremony to present the cocoon.

接着收取茧税，依据各人所占桑田多寡，均摊应献蚕茧的数量。不论贵贱长幼都一样。

Cocoon tax is now collected. Everyone — men and women, old and young — has to hand in a certain amount of silkworm cocoon depending on how many mulberry trees he/she has.

这些茧丝被用来制作祭天地和祖先的礼服。

The cocoon is used to make robes worn by people when they offer sacrifices to heaven, earth and their ancestors.

这个月，天子在宗庙举行"饮酎"之礼，品尝新酒，用乐伴奏。

During the month, the emperor holds a ceremony at which new wines are tasted with the accompaniment of music.

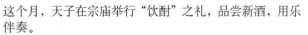

仲夏之月，日在東井，
昏亢中，旦危中。
其日丙丁。其帝炎帝，
其神祝融。其蟲羽。
其音徵，律中蕤賓。
其數七。其味苦，
其臭焦。其祀
灶，祭先肺。

仲夏之月

五月仲夏，太阳运行到二十八宿的东井附近。黄昏时亢宿出现在南方天中。
In the second month of summer, the sun moves to the dongjing constellation. At dusk the kang constellation appears in the southern sky.

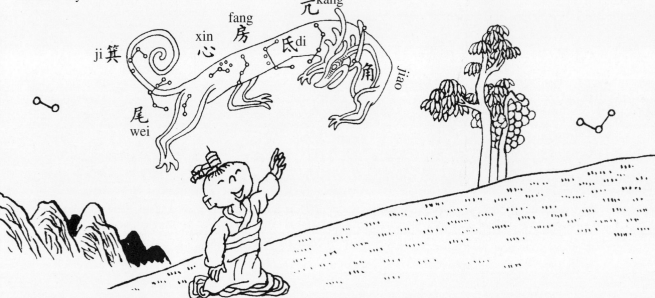

破晓时危宿出现在南方天中。
At dawn the wei constellation appears in the southern sky.

该月之气与十二律中的午律蕤宾相和。
The atmosphere of this month corresponds to the ruibin tone in the 12-tone system.

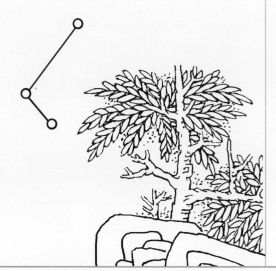

小暑至，螳螂生，鵙始鸣，反舌无声。天子居明堂太庙，乘朱路，驾赤骝，载赤旂。衣朱衣，服赤玉。食菽与鸡。其器高以粗。养壮佼。是月也，命乐师修鞀鼙鼓，均琴瑟管箫，执干戚戈羽，调竽笙簧，饬钟磬祝敔。命有司为民祈祀山川百源，大雩帝，用盛乐。乃命百县雩祀百辟卿士有益于民者，以祈谷实。

节气交至小暑，螳螂长大了。博劳鸟开始鸣叫。蛤蟆却不作声了。
It is now Slight Heat. The mantis has grown; the shrike begins to chirp but the toad has stopped croaking.

天子移居到明堂太庙。这个月，命令乐师整修大鼓小鼓，清理所有的管弦乐器。
The emperor moves to stay in the ancestral temple of the Hall of Brightness. He orders the musicians to check the drums and all the wind instruments and stringed instruments.

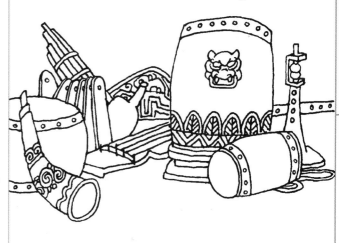

试用文舞武舞的道具。
He orders them to check the supports as well.

这就叫得其时而兴，背其时则废。
This indicates that all living things have their time of prosperity and decline.

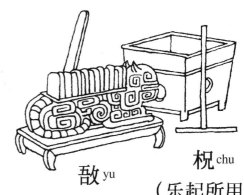

敔 yu
（乐止所用）
(When it is hit, the music will stop.)

柷 chu
（乐起所用）
(Hit it to start the music.)

调和竽笙笆簧等管乐，揩抹钟磬和 柷敔。
To tune the musical instruments such as the reed pipes, bamboo pipes, and clean the chime bells and chime stones.

命令负责官员替人民向山川百源祷告，大雩祭于上帝，用隆重的音乐。
The emperor orders the officials to pray, on behalf of the people, to the deities of mountains and rivers and pray to the supreme god for rain with the accompaniment of great music.

雩：吁嗟声以求雨水之祭。
Pray for rain.

又命各地方官民，举行雩祭。祭祷历代曾造福于民的百官卿士，祈求好的收成。
The emperor orders officials and ordinary people throughout the country to hold ceremonies to pray to the god for rain. They also pray to the officials and scholars of past generations who have done meritorious deeds for the people for good harvests.

是月也，农乃登黍。
天子乃以雏尝黍，
羞以含桃。令民
毋艾蓝以染，
毋烧灰，
毋暴布。
门闾毋闭，关
市毋索。挺重囚，
益其食。游牝
别群，则絷腾驹，
班马政。

这个月，农官献上新熟的黍米，天子用小鸡相配，行尝黍之礼，进樱桃果实，先献于寝庙。
The agricultural official presents broomcorn millet which has just ripened to the emperor who will dedicate it, along with a chicken and strawberries to the ancestral temple.

命令人民不要过早刈割蓝草染布，不要烧灰来煮布，不要在阳光最盛的季节晒布，恐伤时气。
The people are told not to cut lancao (a plant whose extract is used as a dye) too early to dye their cloth. They are told not to use ashes to boil their cloth or dry their cloth under the sun when it is at its strongest for fear of corrupting the energy.

关市行宽大之政，减免税收。
Adopt less draconian policies by reducing taxation or giving people tax exemptions.

重囚给予大些的活动空间，并增加他们的饮食。
Give more moving space to serious criminals and increase the amount of their meals.

不要关闭门户。这样一则顺时气之宣通，二则使暑气便于宣散。
Keep the doors and windows open for good ventilation.

散养在牧场上的牛马妊孕已遂，现在将它们雌雄分养，要把种马系在另外的地方。并公布驯养马匹的方法。
The oxen and horses grazing on the pastureland have mated and become pregnant. Now separate the male oxen and horses from the female ones and tie the stallions to another place. Announce the methods for rearing horses.

是月也，日长至，
阴阳争，死生分。
君子齐戒，处
必掩身，毋躁。
止声色，毋或进。
薄滋味，毋
致和。节嗜
欲，定心气。
百官静事毋刑，以
定晏阴之所成。
鹿角解，蝉始鸣，
半夏生，木堇荣。

这个月，到了夏至，是一年中日照最长的一天。形成阴阳互争的局面，也是万物生死之界。
The Summer Solstice arrives, the day with the longest period of sunlight. It forms a state in which yin (cold) and yang (heat) are locked in a fight and it is the difference separating life and death.

陽 Yang
陰 Yin

君子这时就应斋戒，在家中静心休养，不要急躁。
A gentleman will fast, take a quiet rest at home and refrain from doing anything rash.

停止声色娱乐，饮食要清淡，不要再讲究口味。
Stop all sensual pleasures. Eat light food and don't be fastidious about the flavor.

节制各种嗜好，以平定心气。
Refrain from indulging in your hobbies in order to have a tranquil mind.

百官心平气和地处理政务，不动刑罚，以安然度过阴阳分野的时刻。
All officials should perform their daily routines calmly. They should not administer corporal punishment so as to peacefully pass this critical moment separating yin (cold) and yang (heat).

半夏草已经成熟，可以采挖了。
Banxia, or tuber of pinellia, is ripe and can now be dug up.

tuker of pinellia

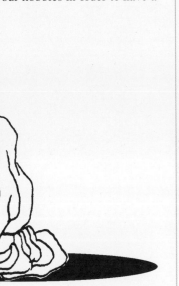

这时鹿角脱落，夏蝉开始鸣叫。
Deer shed antlers and cicadas begin to make a shrill chirping noise.

木槿长到此时开得最繁盛。
Hibiscus is in full bloom at this time.

hibiscus

是月也，毋用火南方。可以居高明，可以远眺望，可以升山林，可以处台榭。

人们可以居往在高爽的地方，可以远眺，以舒散心气。
People will choose to live in high and cool places where they can look out into the distance and relax.

这个月，不可以在南方用火。
Do not use fire in the south in this month.

南方在五行中为火位，重火则伤阴。
According to the theory of the five elements, the south is located in the place characterized by fire. Too much fire will hurt yin (cold).

可以上山岗，也可以住在高敞的台榭之中。
They can move to the top of a hill or live in an elevated, well-ventilated house.

季夏之月，日在柳，昏火中，旦奎中，其日丙丁。其帝炎帝，其神祝融。其虫羽。其音徵，律中林钟。其数七。其味苦，其臭焦。其祀灶，祭先肺。温风始至，蟋蟀居壁，鹰乃学习，腐草为萤。

六月季夏，太阳行至在二十八宿的柳宿附近。
In the third month of summer, the sun moves to the liu constellation.

黄昏时火星(心宿)出现在南方天中，
At dusk Mars (the xin constellation) appears in the southern sky.

（心宿）
the xin constellation

清早奎宿出现在南方天中。
At dawn the kui constellation appears in the southern sky.

the kui constellation
（奎宿）

这一月的节气与十二律中的未律林钟相应。
This month corresponds to the linzhong tone in the 12-tone system.

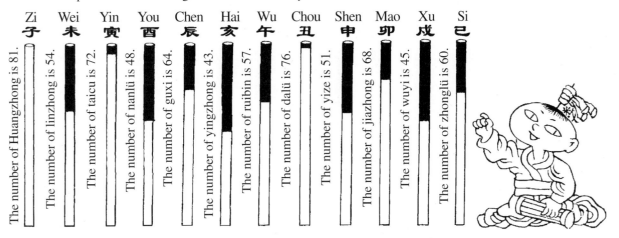

| Zi 子 | Wei 未 | Yin 寅 | You 酉 | Chen 辰 | Hai 亥 | Wu 午 | Chou 丑 | Shen 申 | Mao 卯 | Xu 戌 | Si 巳 |

The number of Huangzhong is 81.
The number of linzhong is 54.
The number of taicu is 72.
The number of nanlü is 48.
The number of guxi is 64.
The number of yingzhong is 43.
The number of ruibin is 57.
The number of dalü is 76.
The number of yize is 51.
The number of jiazhong is 68.
The number of wuyi is 45.
The number of zhonglü is 60.

热风开始吹来。
A warm wind begins to blow.

蟋蟀躲在墙壁里，还未长大。
Crickets are still young and hide in the corner of a wall.

雏鹰开始学习飞行。
Young eagles are learning to fly.

萤火虫得到了夏日的湿气，在腐草中孵化而出。
Fireflies have hatched out of the rotten grass after getting the wet air of summer.

天子居明堂右个。
乘朱路，驾
赤骝，载赤旂。
衣赤衣，服赤玉。
食菽与鸡。
其器高以粗。命
渔师伐蛟、取鼍、
登龟、取鼋。
命泽人纳材苇。

命令渔夫打蛟捅鼍，捉龟取鼋。
Fishermen are ordered to catch flood dragons, Chinese alligators, tortoise and soft-shelled turtles.

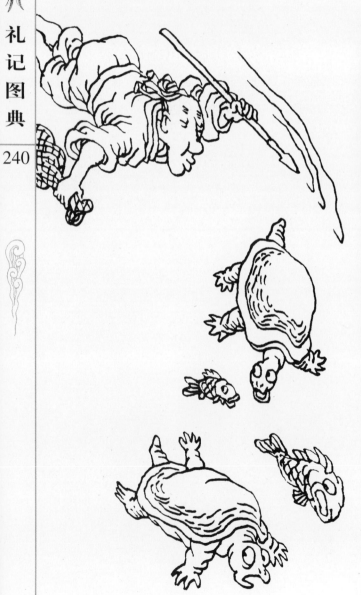

命管理湖泊的官员收缴可用的蒲苇。
Officials in charge of lakes are ordered to collect reeds.

是月也，命四監大合百縣之秩芻，以養犧牲。令民無不咸出其力，以共皇天上帝、名山大川、四方之神，以祠宗廟社稷之靈，以為民祈福。

这个月，命四监(山虞、泽虞、林衡、川衡)之官征集各地按常规应缴的刍秣，用来饲养牺牲。
In this month, the officials in charge of mountains, swamps, forests and rivers collect fodder from all over the country to feed the animals that will be used as sacrifices.

使人民无不尽出其力，来祭祀皇天上帝、名山大川、四方之神，从而为民祈福。
They ask the people to do their best to offer sacrifices to Heaven, God, and all the deities of sacred mountains and rivers to pray for their blessing.

是月也，命妇官染采，黼黻文章，必以法故，无或差贷。黑黄仓赤，莫不质良，毋敢诈伪。以给郊庙祭祀之服，以为旗章，以别贵贱等给之度。

各种颜色的染造，必须依照固有的方法和出处。
The traditions of what colors and patterns to use are strictly followed.

这个月，命令妇官从事染色彩缋。
This month, orders are given instructing women to dye cloth.

黼黻文章：白与黑相间的图案谓之黼，黑与青谓之黻，青与赤谓之文，赤与白谓之章。
The patterns they dye will be white and black, black and blue, blue and red, red and white.

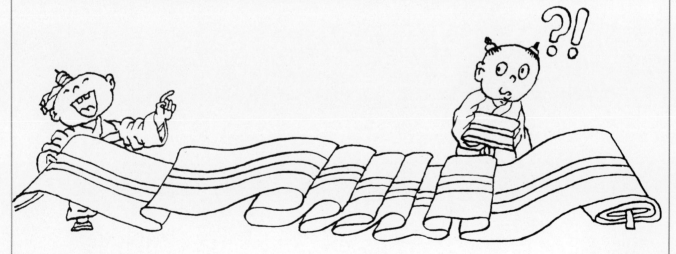

以上种种事宜，不得有一点差错。
The work shall be done without the slightest mistake.

因为这是被用于制作祭祀天神和祖先的礼服。
This is because the cloth will be used to make robes worn by people when they offer sacrifices to heavenly deities and ancestors.

黑白青红，必用真材实料，不许有一点马虎。
Use the best dye without any negligence.

或是用来做旗帜的。
It may also be used to make banners.

或是用来区别贵贱等级标准的。
Or the colors can be used to differentiate people's social status.

是月也，树木方盛，命虞人入山行木，毋有斩伐。不可以兴土功，不可以合诸侯，不可以起兵动众。毋举大事，以摇养气，毋发令而待，以妨神农之事也。水潦盛昌，神农将持功，举大事，则有天殃。

这个月，林木生长最为繁盛，于是命令掌管山林的虞人前往山林巡视，不许有滥采滥伐的事情出现。
During this month, forests grow faster than normal. Rangers are ordered to patrol the forests to prevent excessive logging.

注意不要大兴土木，不可以会合诸侯，不可以兴兵动众。
Do not undertake any large-scale construction. Do not gather the princes. Do not mobilize an army and rally the people.

不可以大兴土木
Do not undertake any large-scale construction.

不可以会合诸侯
Do not gather the princes.

不可以兴兵动众
Do not mobilize an army and rally the people.

不允许发动这些大规模的行动，是因为这样就会扰动该季节的长养之气。

It is not allowed to take any actions on a large scale because doing so will disturb the energy that must be conserved this month.

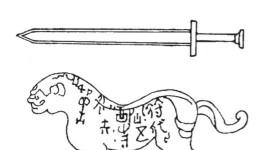

未及徭役之期，不要预发徭役之令，来妨碍土神之事。

Do not give orders for corvée when it is not time for corvée. Otherwise, it will disrupt the affairs of the god of the land.

二十八宿中井宿之宿主水，在未，未月水潦最盛。

The jing constellation, marked by wei, Earthly Branch Eight, is in charge of water. So water will be at its most plentiful during the month of wei.

大帝神农将于这月主持稼穑，培育万物。

In this month, Shen Nong, or the Red Emperor, will be responsible for cultivating all types of crops.

井宿
the jing constellation

所以这时发起大的行动就会违背天意，遭受祸殃。

Therefore taking any large-scale action is against the will of Heaven and will bring disaster.

是月也，土润溽暑，大雨时行，烧薙行水，利以杀草，如以热汤。可以粪田畴，可以美土疆。

这个月，泥土很湿润，所以蒸郁为湿暑。
In this month, the soil is damp. As the sun bakes the earth, steam rises into the air, making the climate hot and humid.

大雨也在东井所主之际依时而下。
There is a downpour when the sun moves near the dongjing constellation.

要在这之前割除和烧掉野草，好让雨水浸泡，以利除草。
Before this happens, people are supposed to cut and burn the wild grass so that the downpour will be soaked up by the grass.

因为再经烈日，水如热汤，草烂后可以为田畴之粪，利于耕田的治理。
When the sun comes out again to heat the rain water, the wild grass will rot and be used as compost for the farmland.

凡土之磊块难耕者，谓之疆。
Land with hard lumps of earth that makes plowing difficult is called jiang.

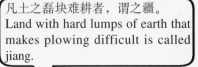

中央土，其日戊己，其帝黄帝，其神后土。其虫倮。其音宫，律中黄钟之宫。其数五。中央土，其味甘，其臭香。其祀中霤，祭先心。

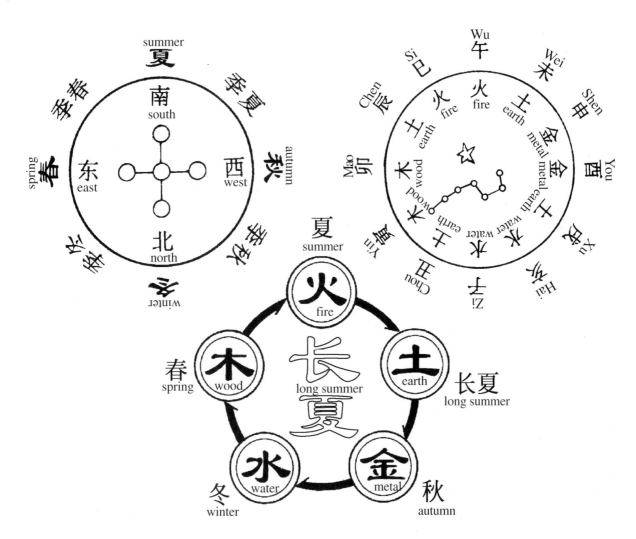

一年的中央属土行，在五行学说中，土寄旺于四时之末，各十八日，共七十二日，除此，则木火金水也是各七十二日。土于四季无时不在，所以无定位，无专气，而寄旺于辰戌丑未之末。

According to the theory of the five elements, the middle of the year is dominated by earth. Earth can be found throughout the year.

未月在火金之间，又居一岁之中，所以特立中央土这一时令。称为长夏，以成五行之序。

Since all the other four elements have their corresponding seasons — water to winter, wood to spring, fire to summer, metal to autumn — earth also has its corresponding season called changxia, or long summer, which comes after summer and before autumn.

其日为十干之中的戊已。"戊"即茂；"已"即起。
The days are referred to as wu and ji, Heavenly Stems Five and Six.

该季的主宰为黄帝，其神为后土。
The ruling king is Yellow Emperor. The governing deity is Houtu.

繁衍的动物是以人为代表的倮虫类。
Animals bred are mammals represented by man.

在五音中是宫，因为宫音属土，又为君，故配以中央。
As far as the five-tone system is concerned, this season is represented by the tone gong. This tone, categorized under earth, is the leading tone and is located in the middle.

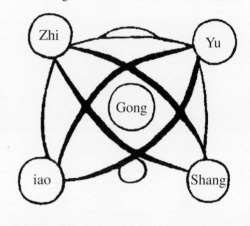

十二律中为黄钟。黄钟本十一月律，因各律皆有宫音，而黄钟之宫，乃众调之首，其声最尊大，余音皆自此出，如土为木、火、金、水之本，故以配中央之土。不取其十二月候气之意，而取其"钟"(此处通"种")意。
Since huangzhong is the leading tone and serves as the base of all other tones just as earth is the foundation of wood, fire, metal and water, huangzhong corresponds to the central earth.

其数五，即古人进行天文观测时所取的东南西北中的方位，称"天五生土"。天五生土，地十成之。其他四时都言其成数，此季唯举其生数，其原由在于四时之物，无土不成。

The number of the season is five, which is also the number for the element earth. The numbers for the four other elements: One — water, two — fire, three — wood, four — metal.

而土的成数，又是积水一火二木三金四之数而成十的。

Adding up the number of water (one), fire (two), wood (three) and metal (four) we get the number of earth — ten.

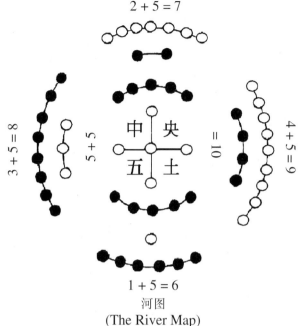

2 + 5 = 7

3 + 5 = 8

5 + 5

中央
五土

= 10

4 + 5 = 9

1 + 5 = 6

河图
(The River Map)

口味是甘，气味为香。祭祀的对象为中雷，也是土神。

The taste is sweet and the smell is fragrant. People offer sacrifices to the God of Land.

祭品以心为上，是由于心居中，属火，在五脏中为君主之官，在五行中火又可生土之故。

The best sacrificial item is the heart, because the heart is in the middle and is the most important organ of the five internal organs (the other four being liver, spleen, lungs and kidneys). According to the theory of the five elements, the heart is categorized under fire which produces earth.

心
heart

天子居太庙太室，
乘大路，驾黄骝，
载黄旂。衣黄衣，
服黄玉。食稷
与牛。其
器圜而闳。

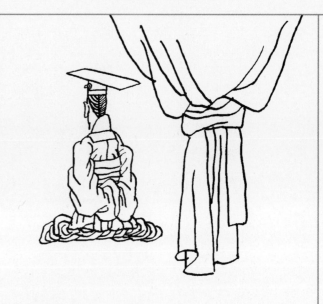

天子移居到明堂正中央的大室。
The emperor moves to stay in the dashi in the center of the Hall of Brightness.

天子乘宽大的车子，驾黄色的马，载黄色的旗帜，穿黄色的衣服，佩带黄色的玉饰。
The emperor rides in a big carriage pulled by yellow horses with yellow banners. The emperor wears yellow clothing and yellow jade pendant.

食物为同属土，性味平和的稷与牛。
The food is millet and beef. Both are mild in nature and are categorized under earth according to the theory of the five elements.

用的器皿要圆而宽大，取土之容物的含意。
The utensils used must be round and big, conveying the meaning that all other things can be made into earth.

孟秋之月，日在翼，昏建星中，旦毕中。其日庚辛。其帝少皞，其神蓐收。其虫毛，其音商，律中夷则。其数九。其味辛，其臭腥。其祀门，祭先肝。

七月孟秋，太阳行至二十八宿的翼宿附近。
In the first month of autumn, the sun moves to the yi constellation.

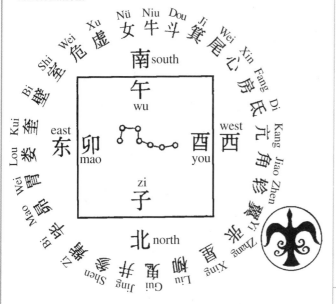

黄昏时建宿出现在南方天中。
At dusk the jian constellation appears in the southern sky.

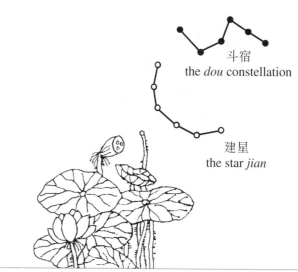

斗宿
the *dou* constellation

建星
the star *jian*

破晓时，毕宿出现在南方天中。
At dawn the bi constellation appears in the southern sky.

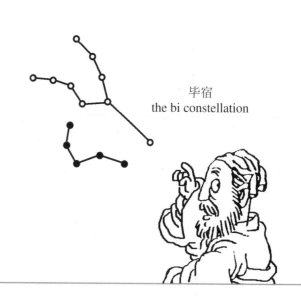

毕宿
the bi constellation

其日为属金的庚辛。
The days are referred to as geng and xin, Heavenly Stems Seven and Eight and both are categorized under metal according to the theory of the five elements.

其主宰为白精之君的少皞，其神为他的儿子，金官之臣蓐收。
The governing deity is Shao Hao, the White Spirit King. Another deity is Shao Hao's son Ru Shou.

所繁育的动物为有毛类。
The animals bred at this time are those with fur on their bodies.

与十二律中的申律夷则相应。
The season corresponds with the yize tone in the 12-tone system.

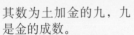

其数为土加金的九，九是金的成数。
By adding up the earth and metal we get the number nine, which is the sum for metal.

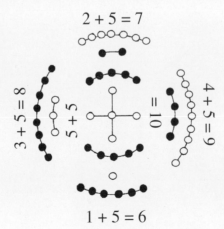

$$2 + 5 = 7$$

$$3 + 5 = 8$$

$$5 + 5 = 10$$

$$4 + 5 = 9$$

$$1 + 5 = 6$$

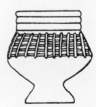

其口味是辛，其气味是腥。辛与腥都属秋金。
The overpowering smell of fish and seafood and its flavor are dominant at this time of the year. Both are categorized under metal according to the theory of the five elements.

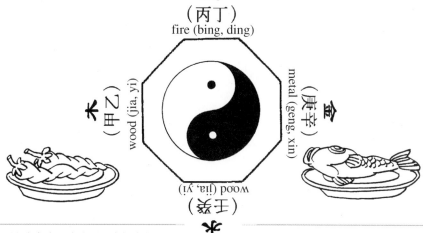

火
（丙丁）
fire (bing, ding)

木（甲乙）
wood (jia, yi)

金（庚辛）
metal (geng, xin)

水（壬癸）
wood (jia, yi)

由于秋阴自此始出，所以这个月祭祀的对象为门。
In this month, people offer sacrifices to gates because they believe autumn starts from the gate.

《黄帝内经》之天门地户图
Chart of the Heavenly and Earthly Gates in the *Huangdi Neijing* (*Classic of Internal Medicine*)

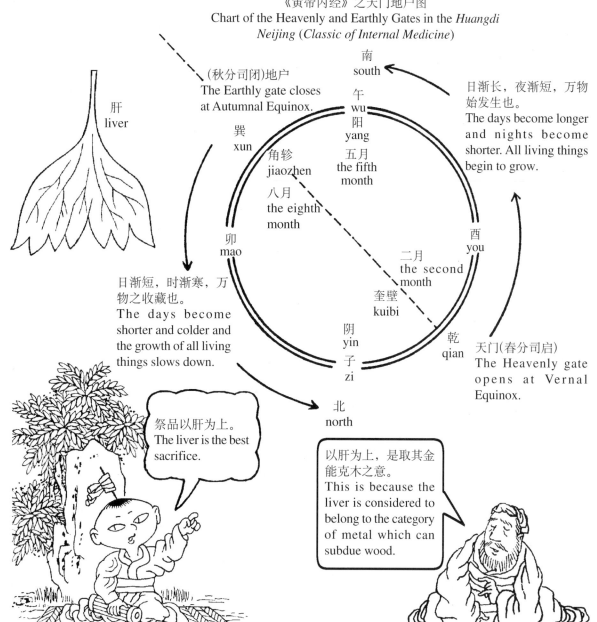

肝
liver

(秋分司闭)地户
The Earthly gate closes at Autumnal Equinox.

南
south

巽
xun

午
wu
阳
yang

五月
the fifth month

角轸
jiaozhen

八月
the eighth month

卯
mao

日渐长，夜渐短，万物始发生也。
The days become longer and nights become shorter. All living things begin to grow.

二月
the second month

酉
you

奎壁
kuibi

日渐短，时渐寒，万物之收藏也。
The days become shorter and colder and the growth of all living things slows down.

阴
yin
子
zi

乾
qian

天门(春分司启)
The Heavenly gate opens at Vernal Equinox.

北
north

祭品以肝为上。
The liver is the best sacrifice.

以肝为上，是取其金能克木之意。
This is because the liver is considered to belong to the category of metal which can subdue wood.

凉风至，白露降，寒蝉鸣，鹰乃祭鸟，用始行戮。天子居总章左个。乘戎路，驾白骆，载白旂。衣白衣，服白玉。食麻与犬。其器廉以深。是月也，以立秋。先立秋三日，太史谒之天子曰：「某日立秋，盛德在金。」

凉风开始袭来，降下白露，寒蝉鸣叫。鹰挚杀飞鸟并把它们贮备起来。

A cold wind begins to blow and frost appears on the ground. Cicadas make their last cry in the cold weather. Eagles catch and kill flying birds and store them up.

杀鸟而不尽食，如国君依时序而实行刑戮。

The eagle kills the birds but saves them for winter, just like a monarch who will not have his prisoners all executed at the same time.

天子移居到总章的左个。

The emperor moves to live in zuoge of the Zongzhang Palace.

乘坐兵车，挂着白旗，穿着白衣，佩带白玉。
The emperor rides in a war carriage flying white banners. He wears white clothing and white jade pendant.

食物以麻和犬为主，麻与犬皆味酸，以顺秋之时气。
Sesame and dog meat are the main food. They both have a sour flavor that matches the weather in autumn.

所用器皿平直而深，取收敛之意。
The utensils used are straight and deep conveying the meaning that things will be stored up in them.

这个月，有立秋的节气，在立秋的前三天，太史要报告天子说："某日立秋，从此时令交到五行的金运。"
The Beginning of Autumn — a seasonal division point — falls in this month. Three days before the Beginning of Autumn, the Grand Astrologer reports to the emperor, "The beginning of autumn is on such date. From that day on, things will be governed by the element metal."

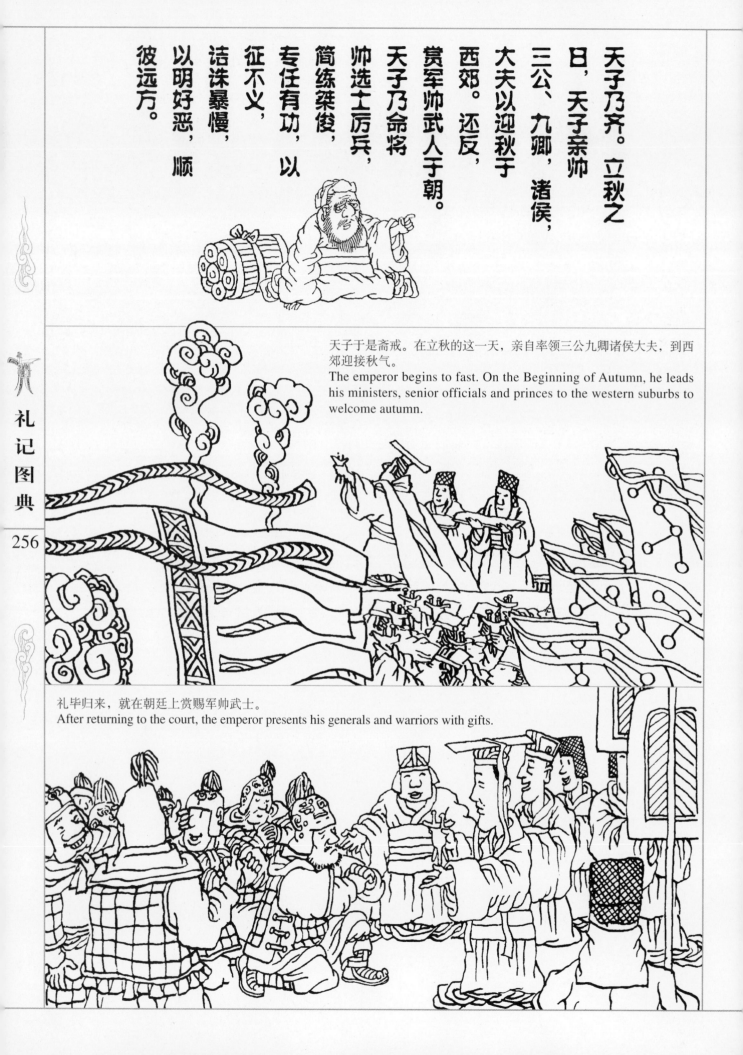

天子乃齐。立秋之
日，天子亲帅
三公、九卿，诸侯，
大夫以迎秋于
西郊。还反，
赏军帅武人于朝。
天子乃命将
帅选士厉兵，
简练桀俊，
专任有功，以
征不义，
诘诛暴慢，
以明好恶，顺
彼远方。

天子于是斋戒。在立秋的这一天，亲自率领三公九卿诸侯大夫，到西郊迎接秋气。

The emperor begins to fast. On the Beginning of Autumn, he leads his ministers, senior officials and princes to the western suburbs to welcome autumn.

礼毕归来，就在朝廷上赏赐军帅武士。

After returning to the court, the emperor presents his generals and warriors with gifts.

继而命令军队的将帅，选拔战士，磨砺刀枪，
提调精干的人，全权付予曾有战绩和经验者，
去征讨不义者。
The emperor then orders the generals to select
capable men and to sharpen their swords. He
gives full authority to those with war experience
and military exploits to launch a punitive
expedition against the rebels.

责罚对下暴虐、对上悖慢的人，用来明辨是非。
He will punish those who despotize their subordinates and
disobey orders from their superiors, to distinguish right from
wrong.

使远方的人能闻风敬服。
By doing so, the emperor exerts his authority over people
in remote areas who hold him in high esteem.

是月也，命有司修法制，缮囹圄，具桎梏，禁止奸，慎罪邪，务搏执。命理瞻伤、察创、视折、审断。决狱讼，必端平。戮有罪，严断刑，天地始肃，不可以赢。

这个月，命令负责官研习法制，修缮牢狱，备好镣铐，禁止不正当的言论，慎重地处理邪恶的行为。有则立即拘囚他。

In this month, the emperor asks the Minister of Justice to study the laws, have prisons renovated and get shackles and handcuffs ready. All heretical opinions are prohibited. Crimes are dealt with prudently. Those who do evil things will be detained immediately.

命令狱官要验伤，观察那些受过轻重刑伤的、骨折的和骨肉全断的囚徒。各种官司，务求公平。

The emperor orders the prison warden to examine the injuries of prisoners who have been subjected to torture and as a result have fractures or broken bones. He wants to ensure that all cases are dealt with in a fair manner.

杀戮有罪，必须谨慎定刑。此时天地间充满肃杀之气，不可以骄盈懈怠。

At this time of year, there is a cold and lifeless atmosphere, so officials must exercise caution when they execute criminals or determine the prison sentences of criminals. They should guard against conceit and negligence.

是月也，农乃登谷。天子尝新，先荐寝庙。命百官始收敛，完堤坊，谨壅塞，以备水潦。修宫室，坏垣墙，补城郭。是月也，毋以封诸侯，立大官；毋以割地，行大使，出大币。

这个月，农官汇报百谷的收成。
Throughout the month, the official in charge of agriculture will report to the emperor the harvests of all grain crops.

天子品尝时鲜之物，必须先进奉寝庙。
The emperor will offer seasonal produce to his ancestral temple before he tastes them himself.

命令百官开始征收税赋，修补堤防，以防水灾的泛滥。
He orders officials to collect the taxes, have the dams consolidated to control flooding.

礼记图典

259

修理宫室，培筑墙垣，补葺城郭。
The palaces are renovated, and the city walls are repaired and strengthened.

这个月不可以分封诸侯，设置大官，也不做割地、出使、赐币等事。
The emperor will not award hereditary titles this month, nor will he grant the nobles fiefs. He will not appoint senior officials, surrender territory, go on an expedition or give gifts.

以上种种，均应于春夏进行，否则违反秋季收敛之令。
All such affairs should be completed in spring or summer. They should not be done in autumn, because they go against the rule of autumn that one should restrain oneself in this time of the year.

仲秋之月，日在角，昏牵牛中，旦觜觿中，其日庚辛。其帝少皞，其神蓐收。其虫毛，其音商，律中南吕。其数九。其味辛，其臭腥。其祀门，祭先肝。

八月仲秋，太阳的位置在二十八宿的角宿附近。
In the second month of autumn, the sun moves to the jiao constellation.

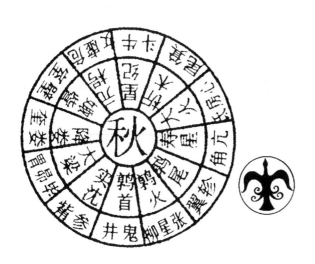

黄昏时，牵牛星出现在南方天中。
The Altair appears in the southern sky at dusk.

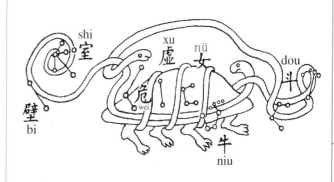

拂晓时，觜宿出现在南方天中。
At dawn the zi constellation appears in the southern sky.

觜宿
the zi constellation

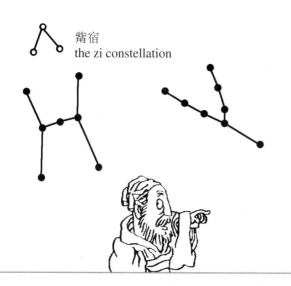

该月与十二律中的酉律南吕相应。
This month corresponds to the nanlü tone in the 12-tone system.

盲风至，鸿雁来，玄鸟归，群鸟养羞。天子居总章太庙。乘戎路，驾白骆，载白旂。衣白衣，服白玉。食麻与犬。其器廉以深。是月也，养衰老，授几杖，行糜粥饮食。

疾风骤起，鸿雁自北回南，燕子南归，群鸟忙着积蓄食物。
A fierce wind blows. Swans, geese, and swallows fly south to warmer climates. All the birds are busy storing up food.

这个月，要养护衰老之人，授与他们几杖。
The elderly must be taken care of this month, by giving them small tables and walking-sticks.

赐给他们糜粥，调节他们的饮食。
Serve gruel to the elderly and regulate their diet.

乃命司服，具饬衣裳，文绣有恒，制有小大，度有长短，衣服有量，必循其故。冠带有常。乃命有司申严百刑，斩杀必当，毋或枉桡。枉桡不当，反受其殃。

于是命司服之官，按规定制作所有的祭服，衣用绘画，裳用刺绣，纹样大小、长短均按制而定。
The emperor orders the official in charge of clothing to make robes used in the ceremony for offering sacrifices. The size and patterns of the embroidery and paintings on the robes as well as the length of the robes must follow the set rules.

日常的衣服尺寸，都根据常法，冠带的样式也不可标新立异。
The size of clothing worn daily must also be made in the traditional way. So must the styles of the hats.

接着再命司狱之官，重申戒令，使所属谨慎用刑，斩杀求恰当，不可有丝毫的枉屈，如有枉屈不当之事，司法者就要反坐其罪。
The emperor orders the Minister of Justice to reiterate the instruction that all court officials must exercise great caution when executing criminals so that nobody is falsely charged and executed. If it were to happen, the person in charge would be prosecuted.

是月也，乃命
宰祝，循行牺牲，
视全具；
按刍豢，瞻
肥瘠，察物色，
必比类；
量小大，
视长短，
皆中度。五者
备当，上帝其飨。
天子乃难，
以达秋气。以
大尝麻，
先荐寝庙。

这个月，就命太宰太祝巡察做贡品用的牺牲，看其毛色是否纯正，肢体是否健全，还要看其肥瘦的情形，身体的颜色。然后根据阳祭(用骍)和阴祭(用黝)的不同，分别牺牲的种类，度量身体的大小、犄角的长短，以合要求。

In this month, the emperor orders the Great Steward and Great Supplicator to inspect the animals that will be used as sacrifices — to check whether the color of their coat is pure, whether they have healthy bodies and legs, to see whether they are fat or thin. They will divide the animals into two groups depending on the purposes of the sacrifice-offering ceremonies. They will also measure the animals, body size and the length of their horns, making sure they satisfy the requirements.

色全为牺，
Animals whose coat is of a pure color are called xi.
体全为牲。
Animals with healthy bodies and legs are called sheng.

以上五者完备，方可献食于上帝。天子于是举行傩祭，以通达秋气。

Only the animals that meet the above requirements will be offered to God. The emperor will hold a ceremony to repel evil spirits and make way for the autumnal atmosphere.

以大麻配犬，先进献于寝庙。

Sesame and dog meat are offered at the ancestral temple.

是月也，可以筑城郭，建都邑，穿窦窖，修囷仓。乃命有司趣民收敛，务畜菜，多积聚。乃劝种麦，毋或失时；其有失时，行罪无疑。

这个月，可以修筑内外城墙，建造通都聚邑。
People can build cities and city walls this month.

挖掘或圆(窦)或方(窖)的洞穴，修葺谷仓。
They can dig round or square caves and refurbish the granary.

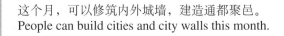

于是命负责官员，催促百姓收藏农作物，存储蔬菜，多积过冬的粮食。
The emperor orders the officials to tell the common folk to store up grain and vegetables for the coming winter.

同时提醒人们播种小麦，不可荒误时日。如有误时的，必处以应得之罪。
The officials also remind people to sow the field with wheat and not miss the date. Those who do miss the date will be punished for their crime.

这个月，白天和黑夜的时间均等，雷声已经消失。
In this month, the length of day and night is equal; thunder can no longer be heard.

是月也，日夜分，雷始收声，蛰虫坏户。杀气浸盛，阳气日衰，水始涸。日夜分，则同度量，平权衡，正钧石，角斗甬。

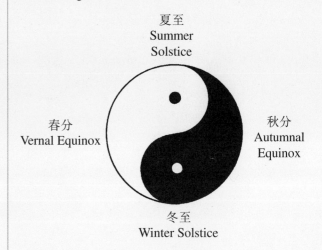

夏至
Summer
Solstice

春分
Vernal Equinox

秋分
Autumnal
Equinox

冬至
Winter Solstice

昆虫增培洞口的泥土，预备蛰伏。
Insects bank up the mouth of their underground holes with earth to get ready for hibernation.

肃杀之气渐渐加深，阳气一天比一天减少，水开始干涸。
Days are becoming colder and the yang energy is decreasing daily. Water is drying up.

当此日夜平分之时，正好统一度量，平均权衡，纠正钧石，校正斗和甬，与春分时同样。
On the day when day and night are of equal length, we rectify the measures. All weights, dou measures, scales and rulers are adjusted, just as they were on Vernal Equinox.

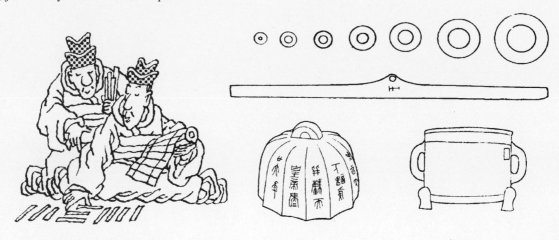

是月也，易关
市，来商旅，
纳货贿，
以便民事。四方
来集，远乡皆
至，则
财不匮，
上无乏
用，百事乃遂。
凡举大事，
毋逆大数，必顺其
时，慎因其类。

这个月，减免关口的稽查和市场的税收，以招徕各地的商旅。通过买进卖出，来便利人民，供给国用。任何公益事项都可实施。

During this month, inspections of goods at checkpoints are reduced in number or cancelled. There are smaller taxes at market this month to attract business from all over the counrty. Trade is encouraged to benefit the people and to supply goods required by the government. Any public service may be offered at this time.

凡是举行劳动民众的(诸如土木徭役、合诸侯、举兵众等)大事，都不可逆反天道。

Any undertaking that requires the participation of large numbers of people (such as large-scale construction, the congregating of the princes or a military expedition) must conform to the Way of Heaven.

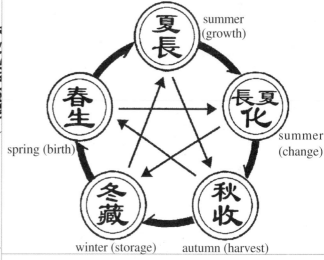

必须顺时行事(如庆赏乃发生之类，刑罚是肃杀之属)，要选适当的时间做适当之事。

Things must be done to conform to the seasons. We must do the right thing (when bestowing gifts, when administering corporal punishment) at the right time.

货：化之以生利；
贿：有之以生利。
Sell the goods for a profit.

季秋之月，日在房，昏虚中，旦柳中。其日庚辛。其帝少皞，其神蓐收。其虫毛。其音商，律中无射。其数九。其味辛，其臭腥。其祀门，祭先肝。

礼记图典

268

九月季秋，太阳的位置在房宿附近。
In the third month of autumn, the sun moves to the fang constellation.

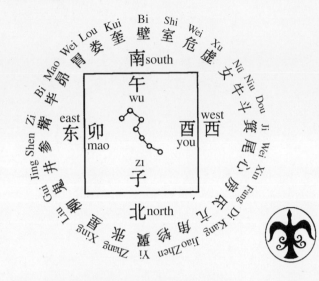

黄昏时，虚宿出现在南方的天中，
The xu constellation appears in the southern sky at dusk.

拂晓，柳星出现在南方天中。
The liu constellation appears in the southern sky at dawn.

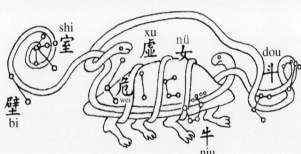

（柳宿）
the liu constellation

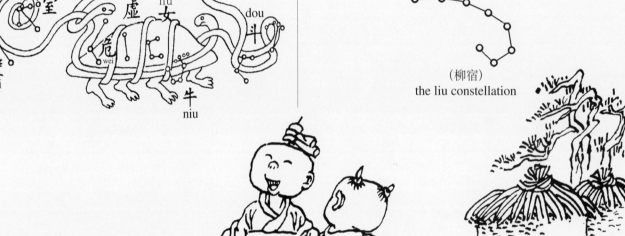

在十二律中是与戌律的无射相应。
This month corresponds to the wuyi tone in the 12-tone system.

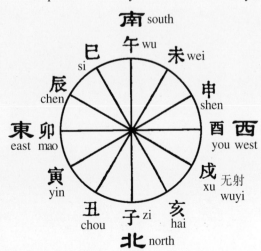

无射之数四十五
The number of wuyi is forty-five.

鸿雁来宾，
爵入大水为蛤，
鞠有黄华，豺乃
祭兽戮禽。
天子居
总章右个。
乘戎
路，驾
白骆，载
白旂。衣白衣，
服白玉 食麻与犬。
其器廉以深。

鸿雁客栖未去。
The migratory swan and geese have not yet flown back to
their original habitat.

鸟雀冲入湖泊河海之中捕食鱼蛤。
Birds dart into the lakes, rivers or seas to catch fish and
shellfish.

菊花开出黄色的花朵。豺在此时也忙于扑杀禽兽，以备
冬用。
Chrysanthemums produce big yellow flowers. Jackals are busy
hunting prey as food for winter.

这个月天子依时序移居到西堂的北偏室。
The emperor moves to the beipian room in the Western Hall.

是月也，申严
号令，命
百官贵贱无
不务内，
以会天地
之藏，无
有宣出。乃
命冢宰，农
事备收，举五
谷之要，藏帝藉
之收于神仓，
祇敬必饬。

这个月，要重申号令，命令百官不分职务高低，都要从事验收的工作，来配合天地即将转入闭藏的季节，而不得悖时施放。

This month, orders for officials, regardless of rank, to check the harvested crops for winter storage, are reiterated. No one shall distribute food now because it is not the time of year.

于是命令冢宰，在农作物都收齐后，登记五谷入账。

When all the crops have been collected, the emperor orders the Prime Minister to register all grain crops and enter them into the accounts book.

把君主名下，籍田的收获贮于神仓，要特别小心，一心一意地去做。

The crops harvested from the land under the name of the monarch shall be stored in the imperial granary with great care.

是月也，霜始降，则百工休。乃命有司曰：「寒气总至，民力不堪，其皆入室！」

上丁，命乐正入学习吹。

这个月，开始有霜降，所有百工艺人等都疲惫了。于是命令负责官员说：
There is frost this month. All the craftsmen are tired. The emperor says to the official in charge:

寒气凝聚而至，人民的体力有所不支，请大家都回家休息吧！
The cold air is gathering strength. People are exhausted. Let them go home and rest.

选择第一个丁日，命令乐正到国学中教习管乐。
On the first ding day, the emperor orders the Chief Musician to teach students in the imperial college to play wind instruments.

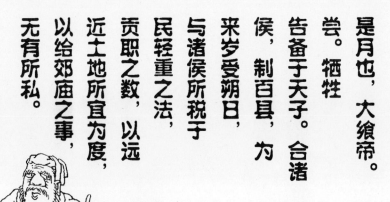

是月也，大飨帝。尝。牺牲告备于天子。合诸侯，制百县，为来岁受朔日，与诸侯所税于民轻重之法，贡职之数，以远近土地所宜为度，以给郊庙之事，无有所私。

这个月，大飨五季的主宰，尝祭群神（先前的大雩是祈求风调雨顺，现在大飨则是对主宰神灵恩惠的报答）。

Ceremonies are held this month to offer sacrifices to all the gods and deities, expressing gratitude to the gods for their favor.

飨礼与尝礼都要用牺牲，仲秋已豢养悉备，到此则告之君主，以备选用。

The animals used as sacrifice in these ceremonies were reared and are available for the emperor to choose.

天子召集诸侯，敕命畿内各县，颁布来年受朔之日。
The emperor summons the dukes. He orders all the counties to announce their calendar for the following year.

诸侯国内的税率，应依其距离的远近和土地的大小而制定。
The rate of taxation of a feudal state is determined by how far it is from the capital and how much land it has.

以此供给郊天祭祖的活动，不得有所保留。
Tributes from the feudal states are used without reserve in the ceremony to offer sacrifice to the ancestors.

小臣那里地窄人稀，又赶上年成不好……
We don't have much land and the population is small. Unfortunately the harvest this year is poor...

是月也，天子乃教于田猎，以习五戎，班马政。命仆及七驺咸驾，载旍，授车以级，整设于屏外。司徒搢扑，北面誓之。天子乃厉饰，执弓挟矢以猎。命主祠祭禽于四方。

这个月，天子举行田猎以教人民战阵之法，并操练弓矢殳矛戈戟这五种兵器。
The emperor goes hunting this month in the open country to teach his people battle techniques. They also practice using the bow, the arrow, the spear, the dagger-axe and the halberd.

颁布驯养马匹的规则，根据它们的毛色和脚力分类而从。
Rules for rearing horses are promulgated. Horses are divided into groups according to the color of their hair and the weight of load they can carry.

命令戎仆及御者让七种马都驾起战车。
Then the attendants are ordered to harness the seven groups of horses to the chariots.

车上竖起旗帜，然后依照职位的高低等级来分配战车，整队排列于猎场的屏障之外，司徒把鞭子插在腰间，朝着北方发誓。
Banners are erected in the chariots, which are assigned to people according to their ranks. The chariots are then lined up outside the protective screen of the hunting ground. The Minister of Land and People, facing north with a whip attached to his waist, will make a pledge.

天子便全副武装，弯弓搭箭，亲自射杀供祭的牺牲。
The emperor puts on his battle gear, draws a bow to shoot the animals that are to be used as sacrifices.

然后命令典祀之官，取猎地所获之兽祭于郊，以报四方之神。
Then the emperor tells the official in charge of ceremonies to offer the animals they hunt to the gods as an expression of gratitude.

是月也，草木黄落，乃伐薪为炭。蛰虫咸俯，在内皆墐其户。乃趣狱刑，毋留有罪。收禄秩之不当、供养之不宜者。是月也，天子乃以犬尝稻，先荐寝庙。

礼记图典

276

这个月，百草枯黄，林木落叶。
The grass withers and leaves fall from the trees this month.

于是砍伐林木用来烧炭，以备冬日御寒。
People cut down trees to make charcoal for a cold winter day.

冬眠的动物蜷曲在土洞中，都用泥封了洞口。
Animals in hibernation have sealed up the openings to their dens with earth; they cosy up underground.

于是加紧清理积压的诉讼案件，不要放过违法之人。
Clear up the buildup of lawsuits. Don't let a single criminal go unpunished.

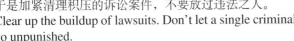

收缴超过俸禄级别的支出，
Confiscate expenditures that exceed the salary of a certain rank.

以及没资格享受政府福利的人。
Deprive people of the right to receive government benefits when they are not entitled to such benefits.

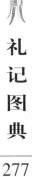

这个月，天子依时以犬相配，品尝新稻，进食之前先进献于寝庙。
In this month, the emperor offers new rice and dog meat to the ancestral temple.

孟冬之月，日在尾，昏危中，旦七星中。其日壬癸。其帝颛顼，其神玄冥。其虫介。其音羽，律中应钟。其数六。其味咸，其臭朽。其祀行，祭先贤。

十月孟冬，太阳行至二十八宿的尾宿附近。
In the first month of winter, the sun moves to the wei constellation.

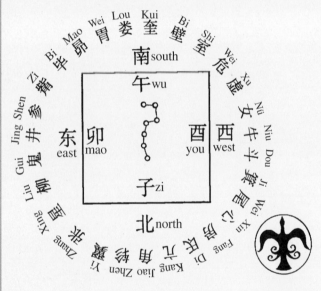

黄昏时，危宿出现在南方天空。
The wei constellation appears in the southern sky at dusk.

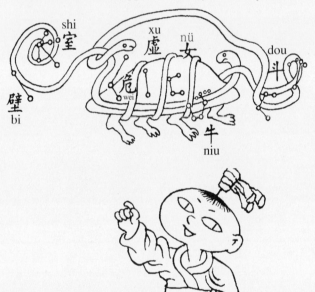

拂晓时，星宿出现在南方天空。
The xing constellation appears in the southern sky at dawn.

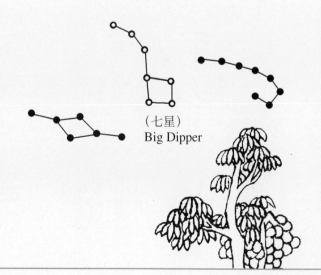

（七星）
Big Dipper

其日为天干中的壬癸。
The days are referred to as ren and gui, Heavenly Stems Nine and Ten.

summer (bing, ding)

spring (jia, yi)

long summer (wu, ji)

winter (ren, gui)

autumn (geng, xin)

该季的主宰为黑精之君颛顼，其神为水官之臣玄冥。
The governing deity is Zhuan Xu, the Black Spirit King, and another deity is Xuan Ming.

颛顼
Zhuan Xu

Xuan Ming

玄冥

繁育的动物为水族中的甲介类。
Animals bred at this time are turtles, tortoises and their like.

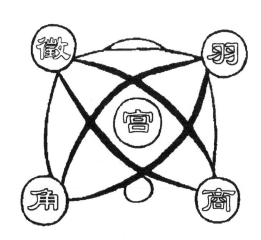

在五音中属羽。
This month corresponds to the yu tone (one of the tones in the five-tone scale).

在十二律中与亥律的应钟相合。
It corresponds to the yingzhong tone in the 12-tone system.

south
南
wu
午
si
巳
wei
未
chen
辰
申
shen
東 卯
east mao
酉 西
you west
yin
寅
戌
xu
chou
丑
亥 hai
zi
子
（应钟）
北
yingzhong
north

应钟之数四十三。
The number of yingzhong is 43.

礼记图典

279

其数为土加水的六，所以六是水的成数。
By adding up earth and water we get the number six, which is the sum for water.

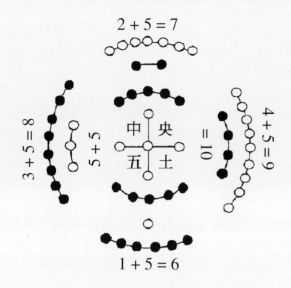

$$2 + 5 = 7$$

$$3 + 5 = 8$$

中央
五土

$$5 + 5 = 10$$

$$4 + 5 = 9$$

$$1 + 5 = 6$$

其口味为咸，气味是朽。
The month's flavor is salty and the smell is rotten.

朽
rotten

咸
salty

祭品以肾为上（春夏秋，皆祭所胜，所以冬季的祭品应为心，但由于中央长夏已祭心，又由于冬主静而不尚克制，所以便祭之以同属水的肾）。
The best sacrificial item is the kidney. (People are supposed to remain in an inactive state in winter. The kidney is categorized under water, so it is the best sacrifice that can be offered.)

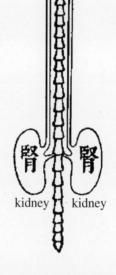

肾   肾
kidney   kidney

祭祀的对象是道路往来之处，以取冬天阴往阳来之"行"意。
People offer sacrifices to the intersections because in winter yin goes away and yang comes along.

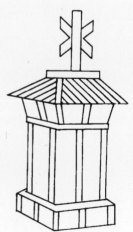

所以在实际生活中，冬季要补阳。
Every day in winter, we need to eat more things that are considered to be yang by nature.

水始冰，地始冻，
雉入大水为蜃，
虹藏不见。
天子居玄堂
左个。乘玄
路，驾铁骊，
载玄旂。
衣黑衣，
服玄玉。
食黍与彘。
其器闳以奄。

此时水开始结冰，地开始封冻。
Water has turned into ice and the vast land
is freezing.

彩虹也由于阴阳之气的变化而隐
藏不见了。
Rainbows disappear as a result of
the changes of the yin and yang
energy.

属于阳物的野鸡不再飞舞，河海汹涌澎湃，仿佛属阴的蛟
龙在翻腾。
The pheasant, which is yang by nature, no longer flies.
Water in rivers and in the oceans rages.

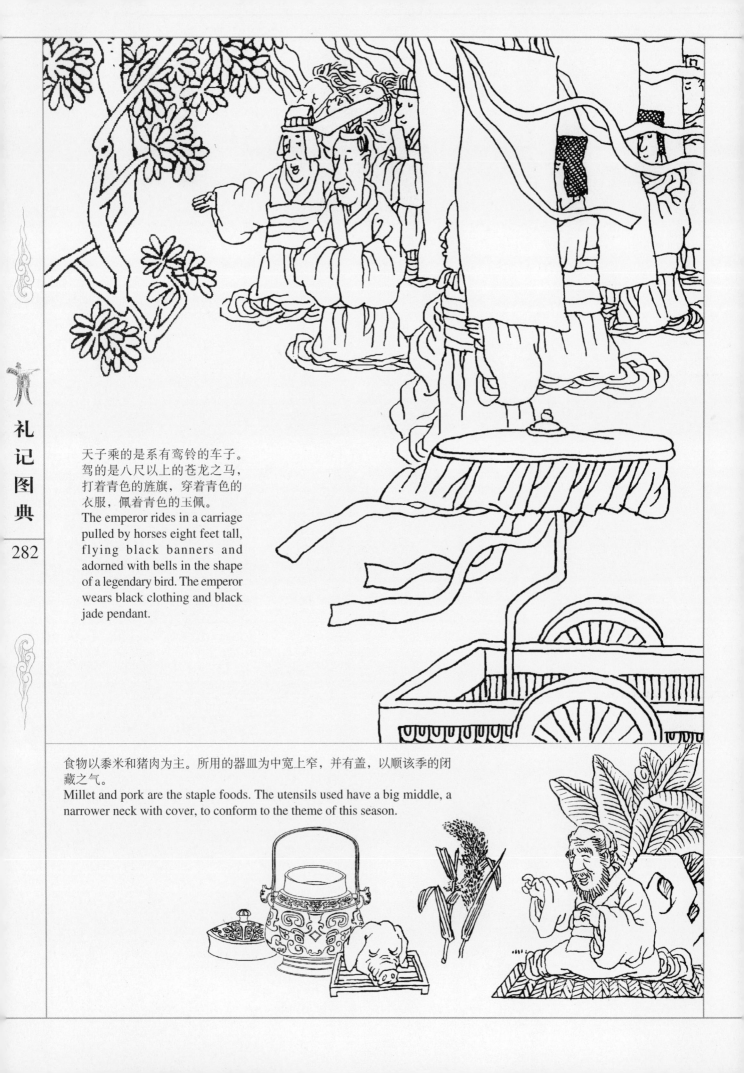

天子乘的是系有鸾铃的车子。
驾的是八尺以上的苍龙之马，
打着青色的旌旗，穿着青色的
衣服，佩着青色的玉佩。
The emperor rides in a carriage
pulled by horses eight feet tall,
flying black banners and
adorned with bells in the shape
of a legendary bird. The emperor
wears black clothing and black
jade pendant.

食物以黍米和猪肉为主。所用的器皿为中宽上窄，并有盖，以顺该季的闭
藏之气。
Millet and pork are the staple foods. The utensils used have a big middle, a
narrower neck with cover, to conform to the theme of this season.

是月也，以立冬。
先立冬三日，太史谒之天子曰：
「某日立冬，盛德在水。」
天子乃齐。
立冬之日，天子亲帅三公、九卿、大夫，以迎冬于北郊。
还反，赏死事，恤孤寡。

这个月，有立冬节气。在立冬前三日，太史报告天子说："某日立冬，从此时令交到五行中的水运。"天子于是斋戒。
The Beginning of Winter — a seasonal division point — falls in this month. Three days before the Beginning of Winter, the Grand Astrologer reports to the emperor, "The Beginning of Winter is on such date. From that day on, things will be governed by the element Water." The emperor begins to fast.

立冬这天，天子亲自率领三公、九卿、大夫到北郊迎接冬气。
On the Beginning of Winter, the emperor leads his ministers, senior officials and princes to the northern suburbs to welcome winter.

礼毕归来，赏赐为国捐躯者，安抚他们的妻子儿女。
After returning to the court the emperor presents gifts to the family of those men who laid down their lives for the country and consoles their wives and children.

是月也，命太史衅龟筮。

占兆。

审卦吉凶。

是察阿党，则

罪无有掩蔽。

是月也，天

子始裘。

命有司曰：

「天气上腾，

地气下降，

天地不通，闭

塞而成冬。」

这个月，命太史杀牲取血涂龟甲与蓍草，占卜吉凶。
In this month, the emperor orders the Grand Astrologer to have the animals (used as sacrifice) killed, their blood smeared on tortoise shell and alpine yarrow to divine whether they will have good luck or bad luck.

检举阿谀奉承和朋比为奸者，判定其罪，揭掉他们的假面孔。
Unmask and prosecute the sycophants and those who gang up to do evils.

这个月，天子开始穿上皮裘。命令负责官员说："天气上升，地气下降，天地之气不得沟通，因而闭塞而成冬天。"
The emperor puts on his fur coat. He tells his officials, "The heavenly air goes up while the earthly air goes down. Since these two types of air cannot interchange with one another, it creates winter."

天
heaven

乾
qian

地
earth

坤
kun

《周易》之否卦
The pi hexagram in
The Book of Changes

命百官謹蓋藏。命有司循行積聚，無有不斂。壞城郭，戒門閭。修鍵閉，慎管籥。固封疆，備邊竟，完要塞，謹關梁，塞蹊徑。飭喪紀，辨衣裳，審棺槨之厚薄，塋丘壟之大小、高卑。厚薄之度，貴賤之等級。

命令百官小心盖藏当年的收成。命令司徒出外巡查堆积的禾稼，不要遗漏。

The emperor orders the officials to store the harvested crops safely. He asks the Minister of Land and People to go and inspect all the crops that have been stored up without missing any.

培筑城郭，警戒街巷，修理门栓，当心锁匙。

City walls are strengthened, streets patrolled, door bolts repaired to ensure the locks work properly.

巩固封疆，防备边境，完善要塞，镇守关梁，堵塞小径。
The defense of borders is tightened, strategically important locations are consolidated, troops are sent to guard the key passes and small paths are blocked.

整饬丧事的规则，分辨丧服的等级。
The rules regarding funeral affairs are tightened. Distinguish the mourning apparel for people of different social class.

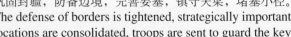

察看棺椁的厚薄，以及坟茔的大小高低。
Check the thickness of the wooden boards for coffins and the size of graves.

使其合乎贵贱的序列。
Make sure all of the above conform to the rules regarding people of different social status.

冬季是一年的终结，丧事是一人的终结，所以于此时整饬丧纪。
Death is the end of a person just like winter is the end of a year. So it is the right time to tighten up the rules regarding funeral affairs.

是月也，
命工师效功，
陈祭器，按度程，
毋或作为
淫巧以荡上心，
必功致为上。
物勒工名以
考其诚。
功有不当，
必行其罪，以
穷其情。

这个月，命令工师呈报工作业绩，陈列所制祭器，考察其样式法度。
The supervisors are ordered to report the performance of the craftsmen. The utensils used in the sacrificial offering are displayed so that people can appraise them.

不许以奇巧迷乱君主的本性。只以做工精致者为佳。
No strange gadgets are allowed because they may disturb the mind of the monarch. The exquisite utensils are considered to be the best.

制作的器物上要刻上工匠名号，用来考证他对祖先神灵的诚意。
The craftsmen must carve their names on the utensils they made as a proof of their sincerity to the ancestors and gods.

如果做工不精致的，一定要追究他的罪行。
Craftsmen who make shoddy utensils will be punished.

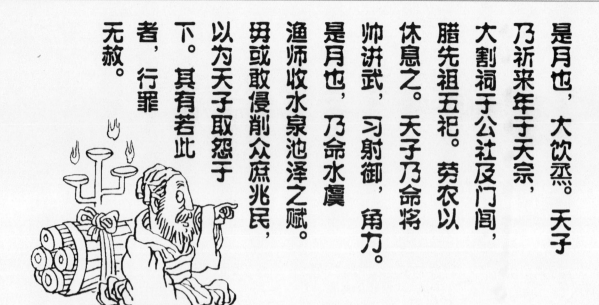

是月也，大饮烝。天子乃祈来年于天宗，大割祠于公社及门闾，腊先祖五祀。劳农以休息之。天子乃命将帅讲武，习射御，角力。是月也，乃命水虞渔师收水泉池泽之赋。毋或敢侵削众庶兆民，以为天子取怨于下。其有若此者，行罪无赦。

这个月，举行大饮烝的飨礼，就是天子向日月星辰祈求来年的恩宠，祷祠公社和街巷。
In this month, the emperor will offer sacrifices to the sun, the moon and the stars to pray for their blessings in the future.

日　月

飨祭先祖和五季诸神，慰劳农人并让他们休息。
He offers sacrifices to the ancestors and gods of the four seasons. He gives gifts to the farmers and lets them rest.

同时天子命令讲习武功，操练射御和较量勇力。
The emperor gives orders for people to practice martial arts and hold archery and wrestling competitions.

这个月，命令主管湖泊的官员和渔师，叫他们收取水泉池泽的捐税。
In this month, the emperor orders the officials in charge of lakes and fishery to collect aquatic products tax.

不许侵害和削减人民的利益，而使天子被天下百姓怨恨。
But these officials shouldn't do anything to jeopardize the interests of the people and make the people hate the emperor as a result.

如果有这样的人，必须加以责罚，决不手软。
Anybody who does this will be punished severely.

仲冬之月，日在斗，昏东壁中，旦轸中。其日壬癸。其帝颛顼，其神玄冥。其虫介。其音羽，律中黄钟。其数六。其味咸，其臭朽。其祀行，祭先肾。冰益壮，地始坼，鹖旦不鸣，虎始交。

十一月仲冬，太阳的位置在二十八宿的斗宿附近。
In the second month of winter, the sun moves to the dou constellation.

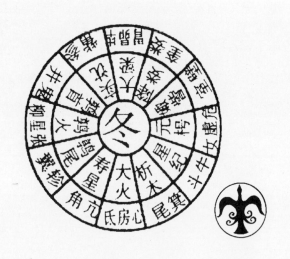

黄昏时，壁宿出现在南方天空中。
The bi constellation appears in the southern sky at dusk.

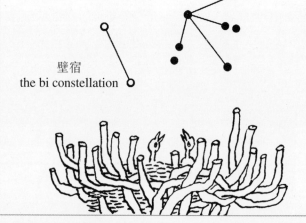

壁宿
the bi constellation

拂晓时，轸宿出现在南方天空中。
The zhen constellation appears in the southern sky at dawn.

鬼 gui
liu 柳
zhang 张
星 xing
井 jing
翼 yi
轸 zhen

这个月与十二律中的子律黄钟相应。
This month corresponds to the huangzhong tone in the 12-tone system.

冰冻得更厚。
The ice becomes thicker.

严寒使大地裂缝了。
The cold weather has caused the land to crack.

老虎开始交尾。
Tigers begin to mate.

夜鸣以求天明的鹖旦鸟停止了鸣叫。
The hedan bird stops chirping.

天子居玄堂太庙。乘玄路，驾铁骊，载玄旂。衣黑衣，服玄玉。食黍与彘。其器闳以奄。饬死事。命有司曰：「土事毋作。慎毋发盖，毋发室屋。及起大众，以固而闭。」地气沮泄，是谓发天地之房，诸蛰则死，民必疾疫，又随以丧。命之曰畅月。

天子依时移居北堂的太庙正室。
The emperor moves to stay in the Imperial Ancestral Temple.

戒饬六军之士，作战必有视死如归的精神。
Soldiers of the imperial troops are told that they must meet their death like heroes on the battlefield.

命令负责官员："凡有土地之事，不可兴作。"
The emperor tells the official in charge, "You mustn't undertake any projects that will involve the use of land."

封闭的地方不得揭起封盖。
Do not lift the cover when it is closed.

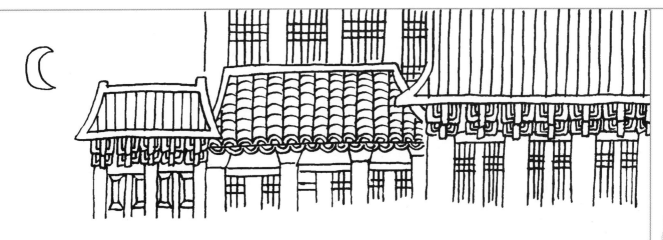

不要将屋室的门窗大开。也不可动用民众。
Do not leave windows and doors open. Do not engage large numbers of people.

要牢固地闭藏起来。
Have all things stored up safely.

因为如果地中的阳气外泄，那就等于放出了天地的储藏。
If the yang energy inside the earth is leaked, it means what the heaven and earth have stored up will come out.

诸多蛰虫因而死亡，人民必然要染上病疫，随之而死亡。
As a result, the insects that lie dormant in the soil will die and people will contract illnesses and die as well.

物极必反，阳久屈而后伸，所以该月又称"畅月"，意即阳畅。
Things turn into their opposites when they reach the extreme. The yang energy will come out after being contained within the earth for a long period of time.

是月也，令奄尹申宫令，审门闾，谨房室，必重闭。省妇事，毋得淫，虽有贵戚近习，毋有不禁。乃命大酋：秫稻必齐，曲蘖必时，湛炽必洁，水泉必香，陶器必良，火齐必得。兼用六物，大酋监之，毋有差贷。

这个月，命令阉人(以其精气奄闭，故名)之长，重申宫内的法令。
This month, the emperor orders the head eunuch to repeat the rules governing the court.

稽查门闾的开阖，谨慎地查看房室，内外的门户必须都关好。
Examine the doors, rooms and houses, making sure that all the doors and windows are properly closed.

减少妇女们的劳作（以顺阴静之意），所作之物也不可繁琐过巧。
Reduce women's work load (women, considered to be a yin force, are supposed to remain quiet during this time of year). What they are working on must not be too complicated or require a high level of skill.

即使是皇亲国戚或他们的近嬖，也不得违命。
The emperor's female relatives and concubines should also obey this order.

于是命令主管制酒的大酋，选择秫米必须饱满，混和麴蘖必须及时，涤洗炊蒸必须清洁，使用泉水必须甘冽，贮酒的瓮罐必须完好，酿造时间必须适宜。

Orders are given to the official in charge of brewing wine: the grains of the sorghum must be plump; the yeast must be added to the sorghum in time; a high standard of hygiene must be maintained when washing and steaming the sorghum; sweet and refreshing spring water should be used; the vats for storing the wine must be in good condition and brewing time must be right.

然后天子命令祭司分别祭祀四海、大川、河流、深泽以及井泉的神祇。

Then the emperor asks the official in charge to offer sacrifices to the gods of the four seas, the rivers, lakes and springs.

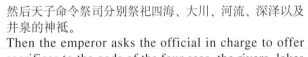
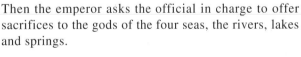

这六个酿造程序，由大酋负责督察，不可有一点差弛。

The official will supervise all wine-making procedures without any mistakes.

是月也，農有不收藏積聚者，馬牛畜獸有放佚者，取之不詰。山林藪澤，有能取蔬食、田獵禽獸者，野虞教導之。其有相侵奪者，罪之不赦。

礼记图典

296

这个月，农民如果仍有不收藏积聚谷物，仍把牛马畜兽散放在外面的，则任人取之而不加以追究。
In this month, if farmers leave their grain crops outdoors without having stored them up, or if they let their cattle wander freely outside the house, then people may get the grain or take the animal away and not be liable to punishment.

山林薮泽之中的蔬菜果实，或是可以围猎鸟兽的，负责山泽事物的官员应指导人们怎样做。
The officials responsible for the forests will tell people what they can and cannot do with regards to the vegetables, forest fruit and animals that people may hunt.

是月也，日短至，阴阳争，诸生荡。君子齐戒，处必掩身，身欲宁，去声色，禁嗜欲，安形性，事欲静，以待阴阳之所定。芸始生，荔挺出，蚯蚓结，麋角解，水泉动。日短至，则伐木取竹箭。

这个月，白昼最短，阴阳互为消长，各种生物因而产生变化。
The days are shortest this month. The forces of yin and yang rise and fall, causing changes to all living things.

有盼头了！
Good days will come.

君子要斋戒，处身之所必须严密。
Gentlemen must fast in a tightly closed room.

摒除声色的娱乐，禁止一切嗜好欲望。
One must abstain from sensual pleasures; put a stop to all hobbies and desires.

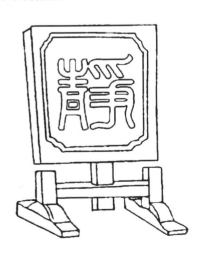

稳定身心，不妄劳作，以待阴阳的消长。
Stabilize the body and mind. Do not engage in any manual labor. Wait for the rise and fall of the yin and yang forces.

芸草开始生长发芽。蚯蚓蜷曲在土中。
The yun (*Cymbopogon distans*) begins to sprout and grow; earthworms wriggle in the soil.

鹿角脱落，水源由于冬至一阳始生而滋发。
Deer shed their antlers and more and more water begins to flow from the source with the arrival of the Winter Solstice and the yang force that comes along with it.

日短到极点，阴盛则材成，可以伐木，可以截取大竹和小箭了。
It is the shortest day. When yin forces are thriving, timber is ripe and can be cut down.

这个月，可以罢免无事可做的冗官，废除没有用处的器物。
During this month, the government will dismiss incompetent officials and discard obsolete utensils.

大扫除。
Throw them away.

堵塞宫阙和门间，修筑牢狱，用以成就天地的闭藏之气。
Seal up the doors and windows and strengthen the prisons so as to follow heaven and earth as they close everything up.

季冬之月，日在婺女，昏娄中，旦氐中。其日壬癸。其帝颛顼，其神玄冥。其虫介。其音羽，律中大吕。其数六。其味咸，其臭朽。其祀行，祭先肾。

十二月季冬，太阳行至二十八星宿的女宿附近。
In the third month of winter, the sun moves to the nü constellation.

黄昏时，娄宿出现在南方天空中。
The lou constellation appears in the southern sky at dusk.

拂晓，氐宿出现在南方天空中。
The di constellation appears in the southern sky at dawn.

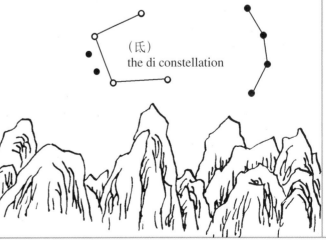

（氐）
the di constellation

雁北向，鹊始巢，雉雊，鸡乳。天子居玄堂右个。乘玄路，驾铁骊，载玄旂。衣黑衣，服玄玉。食黍与彘。其器闳以奄。命有司大难，旁磔，出土牛，以送寒气。

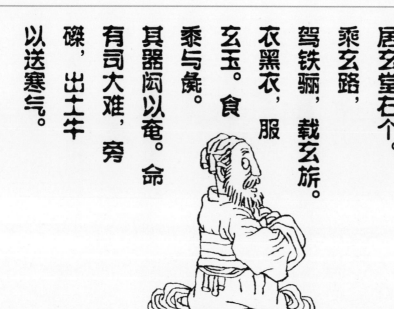

雁开始向北飞，鹊开始筑巢。
Wild geese are flying north and magpies are beginning to make their nests.

野鸡开始鸣叫，家鸡开始孵蛋。
The pheasants begin to warble. The hen sits.

天子依时移居到北堂东北的侧室。
The emperor moves to stay in the northeastern room in the Beitang.

命负责官员举行大傩，在都城四门分割牲畜。并做土牛，以送冬寒。
A grand ceremony is held to offer sacrifices to the gods, on the emperor's orders. Animals are carved up at the four gates of the capital city. People fashion an ox from clay to send away the winter's cold weather.

征鸟厉疾。
乃毕山川之祀，
及帝之大臣，
天之神祇。
是月也，
命渔师始渔。
天子亲往。
乃尝鱼，
先荐寝庙。
冰方盛，水泽
腹坚。命取冰，
冰以入。

膺隼凶猛而矫健地出没空中。
Eagles and falcons glide through the air.

于是结束当年对山川神鬼以及五帝之佐和天之神祇的祭祀。
People bring an end to the first ceremony to offer sacrifices to different gods.

这个月，命令渔师开始打鱼，天子亲自前往察看，在食鱼之前，先进献于祖庙。
In this month, the emperor orders the fishermen to start fishing. He goes and watches them fish. Before they taste the fish, it is offered at the ancestral temple as a tribute.

这时冰冻得正坚实，湖泊中凝结着很厚的冰。天子命令取冰，然后用窖储藏。
The lake has frozen solid. The emperor orders the people to gather the ice and store it in their cellars.

令民出五种。命农计耦耕事，修耒耜，具田器。命乐师大合吹而罢。乃命四监收秩薪柴，以共郊庙及百祀之薪柴，以共郊庙及百祀之薪燎。是月也，日穷于次，月穷于纪，星回于天，数将几终，岁且更始。

命令农官布告人民，选出五谷的种子。
The emperor orders the officials in charge of agriculture to tell the people to select seeds for the grain crops.

使农民筹划耕作之事。修缮耒耜，置办耕田的器具。
The officials instruct the farmers to plan for the cultivation of soil, repair their plows and get other farm tools ready.

命令乐师举行一次联合演奏，然后解散。
The emperor orders the musicians to give an instrumental recital and then he dismisses them.

接着命令监管山林川泽的四种官员，收缴百姓应缴的柴薪，以此来充作祭祀上天、祖先等各种祭祀所用的薪燎。
Then the emperor orders the officials in charge of mountains, forests, rivers and lakes to gather firewood to be offered by the ordinary people as a tribute. The firewood is to be used in the ceremonies that offer sacrifices to the emperor's ancestors and gods.

薪燎，炊爨及夜燎所用之物。
Xinliao, or firewood, was used to look food or burned at night.

大而折者为薪
Xin refers to firewood that is thick and has been cut into short pieces.

小而束者为柴
Liao refers to a bunch of thin sticks.

这个月，太阳回到了原来的位置，月亮盈亏终了，星宿也运行了一周天。一年之数即将告终，新的一年马上就要来到了。
This month, the sun returns to its original location. The moon has completed the waxing and waning and stars have completed a full cycle. The year is coming to an end and a new year will soon start.

专而农民，毋有所使。天子
乃与公卿大夫共饬
国典，论时令，
以待来岁之
宜。乃命
太史次诸侯之
列，赋之
牺牲，以
共皇天上帝
社稷之飨。乃命
同姓之邦，
共寝庙之刍豢。

礼记图典

304

要使农民专于农事，不使他们更有别的劳役。
Let the farmers concentrate on farming; do not employ them to do other corée labor.

天子于是聚合众臣，共同研究国家的法典，讨论四时的政纲，使之适合来年的情况。
The emperor calls the ministers together to examine the country's statutes and to discuss the political program so that it will suit the circumstances of the coming year.

接着命令太史注册大小诸侯，使其如数奉上牺牲，用来祭祀皇天上帝和社稷。
The emperor orders the Grand Astrologer to register the dukes so that they will offer animals used as sacrifices to gods.

又命令同姓的国家，提供祭祀祖先所用的牺牲。
He orders the feudal states that have the same surname as himself to offer animals used as sacrifices to the ancestors.

命宰历卿大夫
至于庶民土
田之数，
而赋牺牲，
以共山林名
川之祀。
凡在天下
九州之民者，
无不咸献
其力，以共皇
天上帝、
社稷寝庙、
山林名川之祀。

又命令小宰排列卿大夫的禄田，以及庶民百姓土地的数目，使其如数奉献牺牲，用来祭祀山林大川。

The emperor orders the Great Steward to register the land owned by other officials and ordinary people. They are required to offer animals for sacrifice to the gods of the mountains and rivers based on how much land they have.

凡是天下九洲的人民都要尽其所能，用于皇天上帝、社稷寝庙以及山林大川的祭祀。

All people throughout the country must do their best to give things that will be used in the ceremonies to offer sacrifices to the gods and ancestors.

图书在版编目（CIP）数据

礼记图典 / 周春才编绘；贺军译.
—北京：海豚出版社，2006.8
ISBN 7-80138-519-5

I. 礼...　II. ①周... ②贺...
III. 礼仪—中国—古代—图集　IV. K892.9-64

中国版本图书馆 CIP 数据核字（2005）第 157330 号

礼记图典

编绘：周春才
翻译：贺　军
社址：北京百万庄大街 24 号　　　邮编：100037
印刷：北京京师印务有限公司
开本：16 开（889 毫米 × 1194 毫米）
文种：中英　　　　　　　　　　　印张：19.5
版次：2006 年 8 月第 1 版　2006 年 8 月第 1 次印刷
标准书号：ISBN 7-80138-519-5
定价：45.00 元